# PRAISE FOR THE AUTHOR

*"As a New York bestselling author I'm always teaching people to follow their passion and to take Action.*

*Jacine is a perfect example of just that. If you're ready to learn the secrets from someone who takes action then…Read This Book Now!"*

**John Assaraf - #1 New York Times bestselling author**

**John Assaraf** "The Brain Whisperer" is one of the leading high performance, success coaches in the world. He is a behavioral neuroscience researcher who has appeared numerous times on Larry King live, Anderson Cooper and The Ellen DeGeneres Show.

As CEO and co-founder, he grew Re/Max of Indiana from startup to 85 offices and 1200 sales associates who sold over $4 Billion a year.

John was also one of the founders of Bamboo/IPIX that went public on NASDAQ with a market cap of $2.5 Billion.

John has written four books including **two New York Times best sellers** that have been translated to 35 languages. He is the creator of the "Innercise" movement and has been featured in 11 movies, including the blockbuster hit "The Secret" and "Quest For Success" with Richard Branson and the Dalai Lama.

He lives in San Diego with his wife and two sons. In addition to being a vegan, meditator, an avid skier, and ocean lover, he loves traveling the world and making some of the tastiest hot sauces using some of the hottest peppers on the planet.

**Today, he is CEO of MyNeuroGym.com,** a neuroscience based company, dedicated to helping individuals strengthen their mindset, so they achieve their goals and dreams… faster and easier than ever before.

# *Just* GO FOR IT

**GLOBAL**
PUBLISHING
G R O U P

**Global Publishing Group**
Australia • New Zealand • Singapore • America • London

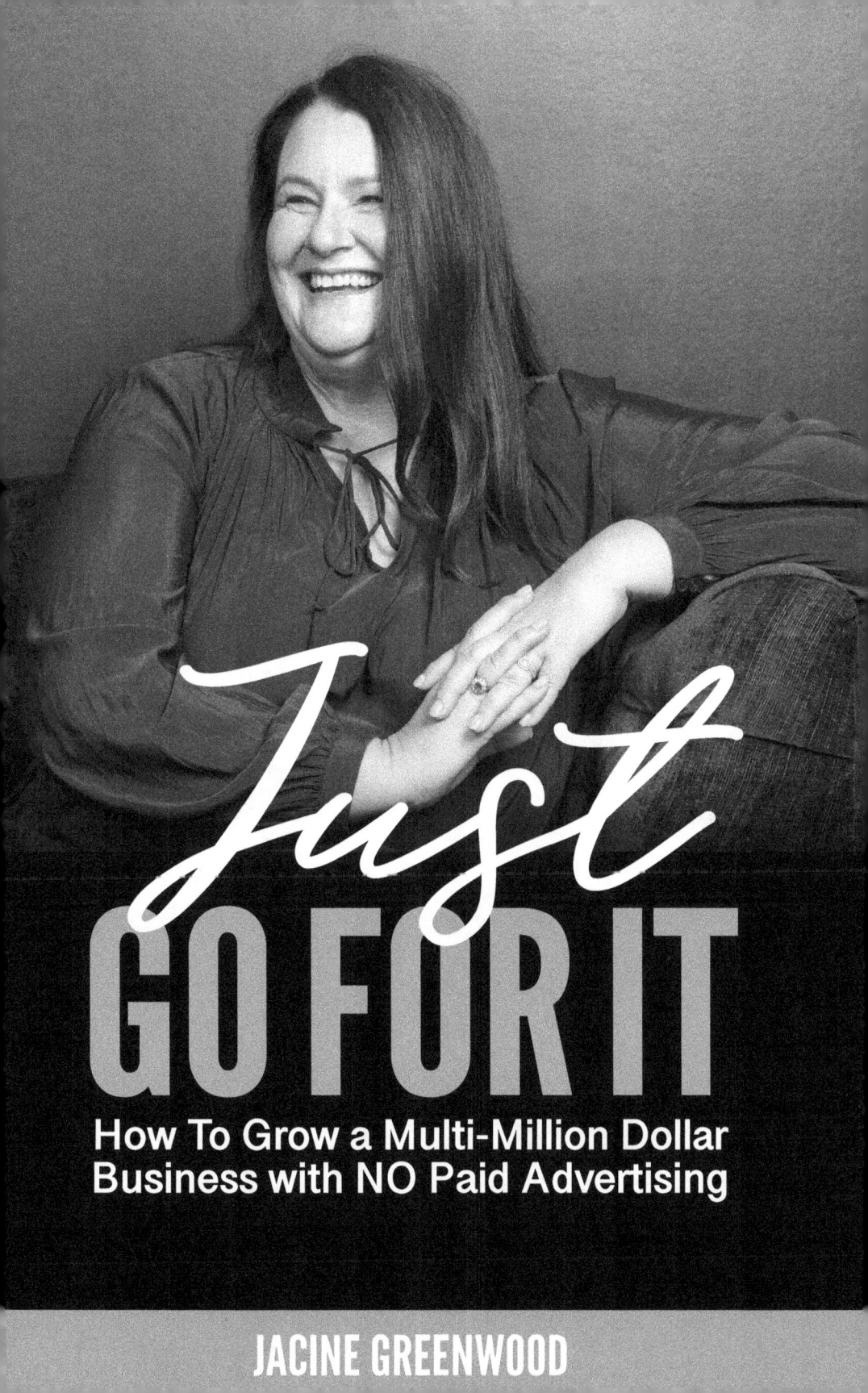

# Just

# GO FOR IT

## How To Grow a Multi-Million Dollar Business with NO Paid Advertising

## JACINE GREENWOOD

DISCLAIMER

All the information, techniques, skills and concepts contained within this publication are of the nature of general comment only and are not in any way recommended as individual advice. The intent is to offer a variety of information to provide a wider range of choices now and in the future, recognising that we all have widely diverse circumstances and viewpoints. Should any reader choose to make use of the information contained herein, this is their decision, and the contributors (and their companies), authors and publishers do not assume any responsibilities whatsoever under any condition or circumstances. It is recommended that the reader obtain their own independent advice.

First Edition 2023

National Library of Australia
Cataloguing-in-Publication entry:

Just Go For It: How To Grow a Multi-Million Dollar Business with NO Paid Advertising - Jacine Greenwood

1st ed.
ISBN: 978-1-925370-07-2 (pbk.)

A catalogue record for this book is available from the National Library of Australia

Published by Global Publishing Group
PO Box 258, Banyo, QLD 4014 Australia
Email admin@globalpublishinggroup.com.au

For further information about orders:
Phone: +61 7 3267 0747

# ACKNOWLEDGEMENTS

It has been an honour and privilege to write this book. As with any major project, there are a number of very special people who contributed to making this book happen. So, I'd like to take this opportunity to say, "THANK YOU".

Firstly, I'd like to thank my Mentor, Darren J. Stephens, who gave me the courage to write and share my journey; for inspiring me to think differently and for elevating my business acumen and skills. Without Darren's guidance, I would not have had the massive media exposure we have achieved. Darren should be called the millionaire maker.

Secondly, I'd like to thank John Assaraf. John was the person who first made me realise what I was capable of. After watching him in "The Secret" for the first time in my life, I realised I could change my destiny. Without that first initial "spark" of hope from John, I would never have become an Entrepreneur. I still don't think John realises how profoundly he impacted my life. I will be forever indebted to him for this. John has been my mentor for years.

Thank you to my children Corrine Clarenwood, Stuart Lowe and Philip Lowe for allowing the entrepreneur in me to grow, knowing I love you more than life itself.

To my husband David Drummond, you are my muse and the love of my life. Thank you for allowing me to follow my entrepreneurial heart and supporting me with each leap I take. I would not achieve half of what I do without your unwavering love and support. You are my everything.

A special Thank You to our publisher Global Publishing Group, and to their excellent team, for your dedication and commitment to the book's success.

# FOREWORD

The book you're holding in your hands at this moment contains some of the most powerful business & mindset lessons available to you on our planet today. I've been profoundly touched and influenced by Jacine's entrepreneurial message in this book and deeply honoured that Jacine has asked me to provide a foreword.

As an international bestselling author and consultant myself, I've had the privilege to consult and work with tens of thousands of people, from presidents, members of a royal family, movie stars and Fortune 500 executives to everyday people from all walks of life, in over 35 countries. I continually strive to help people become more successful and make a difference in the world. As someone who has worked with a huge range of diverse businesses, Jacine's message is very timely and powerful.

We live in the age of information – the most fast-paced era of known history, with the super-highway known as the 'internet' where, with the touch of your computer keyboard or smartphone, you can make contact, and access information and people virtually anywhere in the world instantly.

We have more choices and opportunities today than at any other time in human history. However, we also have more confusion, information overload and less guidance on how to make those choices that can propel us to wealth, success and abundance.

Jacine unreservedly shares her methodology of thinking and her 21 years of wisdom necessary to create a multi-million dollar business without any paid advertising. Jacine is someone who is constantly growing, learning and implementing marketing strategies into her business on her way to becoming a billionaire.

So it is with great pleasure that I invite you to now read Jacine's book to rediscover your true passion, to get clear about what you really want in life and to find strategies to add to your business. In addition, it will help you visualise and tap into new ways of focusing your mind, so you're able to create the extraordinary life you truly desire and deserve.

**Darren J. Stephens**
#1 International Bestselling Author of
*"Millionaires & Billionaires Secrets Revealed"*

www.DarrenJStephens.com

# CONTENTS

# CONTENTS

# CHAPTER ONE
## Just Start

# CHAPTER ONE

—— **Just Start** ——

## Let Go Of Perfectionism

There's a reason why so many entrepreneurs never get started: they're perfectionists. They want everything to be just right before they take the plunge, but that's often not possible. They compare themselves to businesses that earn hundreds of millions and think, "If I can't look like that, I won't succeed". The problem with perfectionism is that it often leads to procrastination, which can lead to stress and anxiety. When we are constantly trying to do things perfectly, it becomes difficult for us to stay motivated and productive. So let go of the need to be perfect all the time.

Perfectionism can be a massive hurdle for people who want to make progress in their lives. It prevents them from taking the first step and doing what they want. It is easy to get stuck in this mindset of "I need to do this perfectly, or I won't do it at all." People with perfectionism tend to procrastinate because they are afraid that they will fail if they take the wrong action.

Perfectionism is a personality trait that is characterised by an excessive concern for correctness and excellence. It is typically accompanied by high personal standards, overly critical self-evaluations, and a strong need for control. Perfectionism can strangle your business and prevent you from moving forward. It can cause you not to act and miss opportunities due to a lack of productivity.

Perfectionism is a double-edged sword. It can be an asset regarding the quality of work, but it can also become a significant obstacle for those with it. People with perfectionism are often seen as self-disciplined and high achievers, but they also tend to set unrealistic goals for themselves and get frustrated when they don't achieve them. They are often hard on themselves and feel like failures if they don't meet their self-imposed standards.

Individuals with perfectionism often have trouble completing tasks because they will spend too much time trying to make sure that everything is perfect before moving on to the next thing. It's helpful to know the signs of perfectionism to recognise it in yourself or others. If you constantly obsess over details, have unrealistically high expectations of yourself, or feel like you're not good enough no matter what you do, there's a good chance that you are suffering from perfectionism.

The first step is to give yourself a deadline for things to be done. Without a deadline, you will spend way more time than is really needed, when you could be spending that time on another project that is helping grow your business.

The second step is to set realistic expectations. Perfectionists are very hard on themselves with standards that are so excessive that they are almost impossible to achieve. Perfectionism, in some instances, can be a driving factor in achieving excellence. There is a fine line between genius and being overly picky. One of the key distinctions is that if you are a perfectionist, ensure you consciously focus on the activities that truly move the progress of your business.

One of the reasons that people can be perfectionists is their upbringing. I grew up in a household where nothing but 100%

or first was good enough. So, when I got 98% on a test, I was asked why I didn't get 100%. It has been part of my driving force for success because I have pushed myself to do better. I have learned how to choose my focus on what to be a perfectionist about. I am a perfectionist about my cosmetic formulas, ensuring they deliver exceptional results and skin feel, so clients rave about our products. I am not a perfectionist about videos and marketing. I would rather get 20 videos out that are slightly imperfect than spend hours editing them and get one perfect video out. Over the years in business, I have found that this form of perfectionism strangles a business. You get rewarded in life for your output. When you become a perfectionist, your business's marketing output is almost zero.

Most successful businesses are founded on a shoestring budget and a lot of hard work. The majority of businesses don't have investment capital and crowdfunding. So, if you're waiting for everything to be perfect before you start your own business, you'll probably never get started. Just remember, everyone was once small when they first started. Just start and go for it. Remember, there is no failure. There is only feedback. If something doesn't work, then don't change the goal; examine what you are doing and then change your tactics or strategy but NEVER the end goal.

## Presentation Counts But Not As Much As You Think.

Procrastination is never more present in a business than the way something looks. When entrepreneurs begin their business or brand, they often want everything to look "perfect". It isn't possible unless your parents are wealthy, or you have inherited it. For most business owners, having a large budget is not possible when they start.

If you don't move forward because you don't like the look of the artwork, the packaging, or some other feature of your business, then nothing will ever launch. One of the critical features to realise is that your business will be in a stage of continual improvement. The website you develop will not be the last one. We have created eight websites in just ten years of business, so get something out even if it isn't as perfect as you want it to be. As you grow your business revenue, you can improve and tweak the appearance of your marketing and business.

Social media marketing is another area where this presents itself. Many people just fail to get themselves out there because they want every video and presentation to be perfect. The person who doesn't worry as much about appearance and just gets out there and starts producing videos will get 20 times more content than the person who wants it filmed professionally and edited. As we discovered, filming and editing consume an enormous amount of time. Unless you are skilled in videography, you will spend considerable revenue to achieve it.

We grew our brand by just getting out there and doing imperfect videos. It also makes you more relatable to your audience. In a world of fakeness, consumers appreciate "realness". It makes you more trustworthy, and they are more likely to do business with you if they trust and like you.

---

*"How something looks is not as important as how it makes you feel."* **Jacine Greenwood.**

---

I started my first brand with very little money. I saved what I earned and invested it into my business as I earned it. I printed the labels for my beauty products on my home computer, which was all I could afford at the time. The labels were not pretty, and the packaging was very plain. The labels were not waterproof, with the print coming off over time. It was anything but perfect. However, it was a start. If I had waited for it to be "perfect", I would have never started. I would have continually wrestled with the belief that not only were my products not good enough but that also I wasn't good enough. These "ugly looking" products SOLD, and my customers loved them. They didn't care what it looked like …. they loved the results it was giving them.

My first brand Eclogite.

*The lesson for you here as an entrepreneur is: Don't let perfectionism hold you back. If you hold a solution that solves people's problems, they don't care tremendously how your solution is packaged; they just want the solution so they can get out of pain. So, ask yourself what problem you are solving.*

That thought of doing a business. It isn't random. Often the crazy ideas you get are a direct insight into what you should be doing. You are being "called" to what you truly should be doing. The more you ignore this invisible magnetic pull, the stronger it becomes.

To be successful, there are some things you do need to get right before launching your business. You need a good idea; a solid business plan; and the willingness to commit to learning as much as possible. Don't worry too much about the small stuff; that can always be fixed later. The most important thing is to take the leap of faith. So, if you are procrastinating and telling yourself that you or your ideas are not good enough, I am telling you just start. You will grow and learn and change, but just start, or the idea will never get off the ground. Even worse, someone else will get the same idea and launch the idea or product before you. The universe likes SPEED!

---

*"Your dream .... your desire. It isn't random. You are never given an idea you are not capable of fulfilling. So go chase it and never give up. Because it is your destiny."*

**Jacine Greenwood.**

---

## Fear Of Failure

Often the biggest fears holding entrepreneurs back is, "What if I fail?". This fear can be paralysing for many, to the point that they don't take the actions they need to and miss many opportunities that could have made them millionaires.

The fear of failing can keep us from trying new things or pursuing our dreams. For some people, the fear of failure is so intense that it becomes a self-fulfilling prophecy. They avoid challenging tasks or give up easily when things don't go their way. They procrastinate doing what they know they should do, and as a result, they never achieve their full potential.

Fear of failure is often even worse for millennials than previous generations. According to Simon Sinek, millennials have been criticised for being entitled and expecting instant gratification but what is less talked about is the root of this behaviour.

Depending on their parenting, from a young age, they had been taught to believe that they could have anything they wanted if they just tried hard enough. They were given participation trophies and told that they were special. As a result, they grew up expecting things to come easy for them. And when they don't, they feel frustrated and let down.

Instant gratification is a defining characteristic of the millennial generation. In a world full of filters and social media, the perception is that everyone is tough and they have it all figured out. When the reality is that most people don't have it figured out at all. Many only show their life's highs, not the pit where they often spend more time. Those seeing this often can't decipher what is "real" and what is "shown to the world" and often compare themselves to unrealistic standards, thinking there is something wrong with them. When in fact, there is nothing wrong with them at all.

They have grown up with technology that allows them to have what they want, when they want it. They expect instant satisfaction when ordering food, watching a movie, or buying clothes. Most of this generation have never learned how to work hard and delay gratification. They've been raised to expect immediate results, and when they don't get them, they feel frustrated and let down. This is especially true when it comes to their business or career. They want to be successful immediately and give up when that doesn't happen. They have never learned tenacity and grit.

I remember my son Stuart, at age 10, feeling incredibly frustrated because he had tried something twice and was not immediately successful at it. He was judging himself on unrealistic expectations, of how "good" he should have been, given the number of hours he had performed the task. Of course, he wasn't going to be good. He had just started trying to learn this skill. His favourite cartoon at the time was Adventure Time. Ironically one of the episodes had the most epic quote I knew my son needed to hear. The quote was, "Dude, sucking at sumthin' is the first step towards being sorta good at something." I downloaded this quote on a screensaver and put it on his computer so he could see it daily, as a reminder to keep going. The truth is that success takes time and hard work. It doesn't come easy, and there are no shortcuts.

**So How Can We Overcome Our Need For Instant Gratification And Achieve Real Success? The Answer Is Simple: We Must Change Our Mindset.**

Many entrepreneurs have the belief that failure is not an option. Failure is a prerequisite for success. There's a reason why so many startups fail in the first few years. It's because founders want to succeed too fast and don't give themselves enough time to learn from their mistakes. It's been shown that the best way to succeed is to fail quickly. That means you must be prepared to experiment and try new things, even if they might not work out. So don't be afraid to make mistakes – just make sure you learn from them as quickly as possible.

Before starting my brand Roccoco Botanicals, few people knew I had another brand called Eclogite. In my eyes, it had failed because it was never profitable. Our highest revenue was $80K per annum, but that had no profit. After my first business failed, I could have given up, as many others do. Instead, I learned lessons from that failure and started with these new lessons. I invested my entire divorce money into my new brand and launched it.

Many famous people have spoken about their fear of failure. One such person is Michael Jordan, who said, "I've missed more than 9000 shots in my career. I've lost almost 300 games. 26 times, I've been trusted to take the game-winning shot and missed. I've failed over and over and over again in my life. And that is why I have succeeded." This quote speaks to the power of resilience - the ability to keep going even when it seems impossible or when you look in the face of no visible progress.

There are many ways to overcome the fear of failure. Here are some steps that may help you get started:

1. The first is to understand precisely what fear of failure is and why it can exist. There are many reasons why it can occur. Traumatic experiences can create fear, so the individual out of fear stays small because they don't want to experience it again. You may have been raised in an environment where success was emphasised over everything else. This was the environment I was raised in— where being placed second was deemed not good enough. I was always asked why I didn't come first. Once you understand the root cause of your fear, it will be easier to address it.

2. Acknowledge your fear and accept it for what it is. You can't change what you are not aware of. Acknowledging that it exists is the first step. Identify what your triggers are. Every time I take a huge step where I put myself out there, I feel nauseous to the point that I want to vomit. It is my "sign" that I am not in my comfort zone. Instead of resisting this now, I welcome it, because it means I am playing a bigger game and that massive growth will follow. Don't try to ignore or suppress your feelings; simply acknowledging them is the first step towards overcoming them.

   Feel them and notice where the emotions sit in your body. They are often in your stomach, solar plexus, or chest. Allow the emotion to be felt, and you will find that after about 60 seconds of really feeling into the emotion, it goes away. If you keep suppressing that emotion, it will keep ruling your life and stop you from reaching your potential. When you allow the emotion to process, it doesn't surface again.

3. Initially, when you are starting, the intelligent thing to do is to set realistic goals for yourself and take small steps towards achieving them. This is instrumental in building confidence in your abilities and belief in yourself. When you first start, you lack confidence in your ability. I certainly didn't feel confident when I first began. I felt inferior when I first started my brand but despite that feeling of not being good enough. I persisted and each success built upon the previous one. You will eventually be okay with the fear and move through it each time you feel it. It is a myth that those who are successful don't feel fear. We still feel it just as much; we just don't let it control us.

To achieve something great, you have to be willing to risk everything. You have to want it with every part of your soul. You must be willing to put yourself out there and take chances. Sometimes, you'll fail but that's okay, because failure is how you learn and grow. So don't be afraid to fail. Don't be afraid to make mistakes. Just keep moving forward, and don't give up on your dreams.

---

*"When you want to succeed as bad as you want to breathe, then you'll be successful."* **Eric Thomas**

---

## Imposter Syndrome

Imposter syndrome is a term used to refer to high-achieving individuals who cannot internalise their accomplishments. The term is used in both the workplace and academia and was first coined by clinical psychologists Dr Pauline Rose Clance and Suzanne Imes in 1978. They defined imposter syndrome as "a common form of self-sabotage" that "affects high-achieving individuals who are unable to internalise their accomplishments."

Individuals with imposter syndrome often display low self-confidence, feelings of inadequacy, fear of being exposed as a fraud, and an inability to take credit for successes. Imposter syndrome can be found in all industries, from academia to entrepreneurship. It can be especially prevalent among entrepreneurs, women, and minorities. For many entrepreneurs, this feeling can be crippling. It can keep them from taking risks and pursuing their dreams. Often it comes from comparing themselves to others.

Imposter syndrome is pervasive. Studies have shown that nearly 80% of people will experience imposter syndrome at some point in their lives. I have felt this numerous times throughout my business growth, including in 2022.

When starting your business, it's easy to feel like an imposter. You might look at successful entrepreneurs and wonder how they could possibly be as successful as they are. Do they have some magical power that you don't have? The truth is that most successful entrepreneurs have battled with Imposter Syndrome at some point in their careers. They've doubted their abilities and questioned whether they're cut out for this whole entrepreneurship thing. They are human, just like you, and they also have the same fears you are now experiencing. So, know that you are in good company if you feel like that. You are not the only one who has felt like that because I did too.

In March of 2022, I had imposter syndrome again. I went to enter a competition for cosmetic innovation, and once I viewed the requirements for testing and information, I hesitated and did not continue with the application. I didn't feel worthy or good enough to enter, so I sat on the entry, doing nothing. I received an email the day before the competition closed, and I suddenly found the courage to enter with just one day's notice. It was tremendous pressure to get all the information together in one day. I entered, and my first thought was, "Well, you don't stand a chance. Just take it as an opportunity to learn Jacine."

You can imagine my shock when the email landed in my inbox saying we were in the finals to be judged in New York and my further shock when I was notified that I had won a worldwide competition for cosmetic innovation. Never in my wildest dreams did I think I was capable of what I pulled off. It taught me that I am much more intelligent and innovative than I give myself credit for. We often put ourselves down with our capabilities. Many of us grew up with "Don't be a showoff". We have learnt at an early age to downplay our success. By owning your success, you permit others to shine brighter.

As my business rapidly grew, so did our staffing requirement. As a business owner, I didn't know a thing about managing people. At one point, I didn't know what I was doing. It was much easier managing five staff than it was twenty staff. As managing my team became more complex, there started to become a gap in my ability. There were a few years when I felt entirely out of my depth. However, I took the time to learn how to manage successfully because I knew that my business growth would be capped if I didn't. I engaged mentors who could help me successfully recruit the right staff and show me how to manage them, so I was getting the best out of each staff member and playing to their strengths.

The ability of my business to grow was directly linked to my ability to grow mentally and emotionally. What sets successful entrepreneurs apart is their ability to push through these doubts and keep moving forward. They know that Imposter Syndrome is just a mental hurdle they must overcome, and they refuse to let it hold them back. It's normal to feel like you're not good enough. The key is to remember that everyone feels this way sometimes. And if you keep learning and growing, you'll eventually feel more confident in your abilities.

# CHAPTER TWO

— Your "Why" Is Everything —

# CHAPTER TWO

## — Your "Why" Is Everything —

Why did you start your business? Or why are you thinking of starting your business? The importance of "your why" in business cannot be overstated. Your why is the reason you started your company in the first place. It's what drives you to keep going when things get tough. The real reason you started your business, "your why" is what gives you energy and makes you so excited to bound out of bed every morning and embrace the day.

Successful business owners have a strong sense of why they started their businesses. This reason is something that the person believes in and is willing to stand up for. Even if it means not making as much money as they could have otherwise made or giving up some other benefit that might have been available to them had they chosen another career path. Their "why" lights them up and fulfils them on a level that could never be achieved with any other way of earning income. What is it that makes your heart sing and you come alive?

---

*"Martin Luther King did not say, 'I have a mission statement.'"* — **Simon Sinek**

---

Did you start your business just to make money? Ask yourself, "Would you still do what you are doing if you won millions of dollars?" If the answer is, "Yes," then the likelihood is that you will be successful. If you were just starting a business to make money the chances of it being successful are slim because growing a business isn't easy. Without solid internal motivation to continue you will give up when the going gets tough.

Sometimes people start businesses hoping to make money but they aren't genuinely committed to what they are doing and the moment they hit a challenge, they fold. One in three new small businesses in Australia fails in their first year of operation. I have also seen this first-hand with many entering the business world and giving up quickly. These businesses often don't even have overheads yet the sheer lack of progress makes them give up. They don't have a business plan and have no experience. They fail to get a mentor to help them and enter business with a limited budget, often underestimating the business's cost. Their business exists for no reason other than wanting to earn money; when they don't earn it quickly, they just give up.

If I were to view the average business website, it is all about their qualifications and not about why they went into business. This type of marketing doesn't engage people's emotions and is appealing simply to the logical brain. Whilst we like to believe that people are logical, they are not. Humans are emotional creatures and we justify our emotional decisions with logic, especially with sales. This type of marketing also fails to differentiate the business from other competitors that are in the same category as them. Customers are not emotionally engaged so they choose based on price alone.

Imagine you had the choice of going to two skin clinics. One business has an about page that shares its qualifications and industry experience. The other business shares their journey and what drove them to open their business. They share how they overcame their skin challenges. Which one do you think you are going to go to? Most people will go to someone who understands them emotionally. There is nothing like knowing someone has been through what you are going through emotionally to enable a rapid and quick emotional connection. People buy from people they trust. When you share your journey from the heart it builds trust.

---

*"No sentence can be effective if it contains facts alone. It must also contain emotion, image, logic and promise."*
**Eugene Schwartz**

---

When I started my Roccoco Botanicals business it was because of my own personal skin challenges. I just wanted to help people. I didn't want others to experience my pain and embarrassment. My driving motivation wasn't money but the genuine desire to help people get out of pain. Having experienced the emotional trauma of having a skin condition you couldn't hide, I knew first-hand how much it affected your self-esteem. I grew up having to choose my clothes based on how bad my back was breaking out. I avoided any tops with shoestring straps ensuring I was covering up my back. It affects your self-esteem massively. It was not until I was 40 that I felt beautiful and had the confidence to look at myself in a public bathroom with other women around me. I had always been so self-conscious of my appearance.

For the first five years of business I barely paid myself anything. In fact, my staff earned more than I did. To the outside world the perception from my clinic owners was that I was making massive amounts of money. Little did they realise I wasn't. Seven times I wanted to quit. Seven times I felt like just giving up and stopping. There were times when I asked myself, "Why are you doing this?" The answer that always came back was that I felt "called" to do what I was doing. I felt it was my gift to give to the world and that I was meant to reach my full potential. The more I reached my full expression, the more people I would be able to help. This driving force kept me going even when I felt like giving up.

Every successful business has a "why" which is much more than just making money. At its core, your business "why" is the reason you get out of bed in the morning and do what you do. This passion drives you to push through the tough times and keep going when things get tough. Your business "why" sets you apart from your competitors and makes you shine in the marketplace. It motivates your team and gets them excited about coming to work every day.

Many staff members are more interested in working for a company where they feel they are contributing to something more significant. I have had the experience of staff members who apply to work with us who are even prepared to take a pay cut because they know they will feel more emotionally fulfilled. This can be more important than earning lots of money. Simply put, your business "why" is what makes you unique and special - and that's what ultimately will help you achieve success.

Every "why" has a story. Your business is no different. Sharing the story of why you started your business is one of the most potent ways to connect with your customers and inspire them to support you. After all, people don't just buy products or services - they buy into the belief that they are supporting something larger than themselves. When you share the story of your business you give people a chance to believe in something bigger and be a part of something special. In doing so you create loyalty and build relationships that will last a lifetime.

When you have clarity on your business "why", something more tangible than just money, your customers can sense it and come through with every interaction with your business. It becomes easier to make tough decisions because every decision is now filtered through your values and if the decision doesn't align with your overall vision and goals the answer is always no. There have been times when I was not making the best decisions for the company out of fear of upsetting people. I had to bring it back to the purpose of my business and my "why". I wanted to impact as many lives as possible. It has always been about the end goal and my vision.

Ask yourself, "Why you are doing your business? Would you continue to do this if you won the lotto tomorrow?" If the answer is, "No," you are not emotionally invested in your actions. I can confidently answer that if I won 100 million tomorrow, it wouldn't change a thing. I would be at work still doing what I love to do. Find what you are passionate about and discover the activity or thing you would do all day if you were allowed. That is what you should be doing.

The challenge is that many people throw away their talent because they think they cannot earn an income. So they make a career they believe they can earn money from instead of allowing their natural talents to surface. They fail to realise that when you love something it is impossible not to become a master of the subject or skill. Masters get paid more and command a higher fee because money always follows mastery, and very few become masters.

## The Law Of Gestation And The Law Of Attraction

Many supposed "overnight successes" are anything but. Many of these businesses worked for years behind the scenes to achieve the level of growth and impact they have. The challenge is that most people never see this. In 2022, my brand became very well-known, and to those who hadn't followed my company's journey, it appeared as if it was overnight. It was anything but overnight.

Closely tied into your "why" is another law called the Law of Gestation. The Law of Gestation states that it takes time for an idea to gestate and mature before it can be fully realised. This law is often applied in business as it takes time for a business to research, develop and launch a new product or service. Even after a business has launched a new offering it can take months or even years to achieve widespread success. While the law of gestation may seem like common sense, it is often overlooked in the business world. This can lead to unrealistic expectations and disappointment when a new business doesn't immediately take off.

A farmer doesn't plant a seed expecting a tree the next day. For the seed to grow and take root, the soil requires preparation, just like your mind may require preparation and fertilisation for ideas to germinate. Business is no different. It requires constant tending before you may see growth. It is well known that a human baby takes 40 weeks to come to gestation. An elephant takes 645 days to give birth. A chicken only takes 21 days. Nobody goes up to a pregnant woman at 12 weeks and says, "where is the baby?" Yet many business owners and entrepreneurs become impatient. They wonder when things will come together and when they will see success. When growing a business there is often no predetermined time frame to see fruit. Each business is different, with no certainty of when you will see success. Your "why" becomes even more important as a driving force to keep you motivated.

---

*"The reason why people don't succeed is because they are not willing to do the work."* **Jacine Greenwood**

---

Nevertheless, the Law of Gestation is an important principle to keep in mind when starting any new venture. By being patient and giving an idea time to grow, you increase your chances of achieving long-term success. Rome wasn't built in a day and neither are most businesses. So don't get discouraged if things aren't moving as quickly as you'd like. Just keep working consistently on your business and eventually you'll see the fruits of your labour.

Initially, I drew no money from my business. It was over five years before I drew a solid wage. I literally was working for nothing. It took me nine years to even get a profit and it was a paper profit at that. It wasn't in my bank account. I wasn't bothered because I knew that good things take time to come to fruition. I also wasn't doing it for money; I felt compelled and drawn to do it. It was an unrelenting pulling of my soul that became impossible to ignore. Sometimes I wanted to quit but my vision wouldn't let me quit because I believed I would succeed. So I never gave up.

So many just give up because they try for 12 months and quit when they don't see the results they want. The challenge is that they never gave the business long enough to develop roots and never had a compelling reason for their business. The majority simply started because they thought they could earn more than working in a job. They got dazzled by the possibility of earning more money, and they didn't have anything to keep them going when it got tough.

The Law of Attraction is closely tied to the Law of Gestation. Many people have used this law for centuries to achieve their dreams and goals. Some people think this law only applies to positive things and not negative things but this isn't true because whatever energy we put into the world will be what we receive back in our lives. Whatever you focus on, you get more of it. If you focus on things to be grateful for you will get more of them and if you focus on what is going wrong there will be more things to worry about.

The Law of Attraction states that one's thoughts, feelings and actions must be aligned to attract what one wants. This means that if you want something in your life you must be able to visualise it and feel it as if it were already there. When you first start this isn't easy to do. I remember visualising being wealthy and then I would look at my bank account and one part of my brain screamed "bullshit" at me. It took repetition and practice to be able to master it. The more I practiced the more vivid my vision became. I learnt very early in business that if my bank account was low, panicking about it just made it worse. It was like I turned off the money tap. When I focused on abundance, pretended I had money, and turned my focus to wealth, money flowed and the situation completely turned around.

Albert Einstein said, "Imagination is everything. It is the preview to life's coming attraction." What does this mean? Every thought you have is bringing that which you desire towards you. The more you imagine and visualise what you want, the faster it comes to you. Some people find this harder to do than others. As a child, you had no trouble daydreaming. If you are struggling with daydreaming or visualising, practise. It gets easier.

The often-overlooked part of the Law of Attraction is that you do need to take action towards that which you desire. It isn't only action … it is MASSIVE action. You can't meditate about having a million dollars and think it will fall out of the sky. Instead you will get a million-dollar idea. It is up to you to act on this idea and put in the effort to bring it to fruition. When you are in alignment, everything just flows smoothly.

You need to think about every task or activity your logical brain tells you to do and start doing. Just start. The way the Universe unfolds things requires you to start doing something. It may be just an inspiration to follow a hunch but do it because that one hunch leads to another connection and before you know it  success is at your doorstep.

# CHAPTER THREE

—Brilliance Is Created Under Pressure—

# CHAPTER THREE

## — Brilliance Is Created Under Pressure —

One of the things I learnt as I surrounded myself with other successful business owners is that they all had one trait in common. Sheer grit, determination and resilience were their strengths. Resilience is crucial for growing a business. All business owners will be thrown curve balls at some point in their business. Being able to pick yourself up after being knocked down or sideways is crucial. Over my years in business I have learnt many lessons regarding resilience and mindset.

**Lesson One - It is not what happens to you that determines success. It is how you respond to it.**
It is easy to remain positive when everything is going right, but what about when it isn't? This is when the true nature of a person is revealed. It is easy to use things as an "excuse" for why you can't do something. However, it is just that ... an excuse. You can either keep using your excuses or you can find solutions. What are you choosing to focus on?

On February 22nd, 2014, my life as I knew it started to crumble. When the discs in my back collapsed I could have said I could do nothing. I chose not to have a medical condition define who I was. I was not "my condition". My bright, shining, bubbly self was still inside the heavy veil of pain. The pain would wipe me out so much that I slept from midday to nearly 3 pm daily. I had to adjust my routine and work with what I could and not what I couldn't do.

I felt gutted as I had to close my skincare business. Unable to hold a pair of tweezers, I felt my body was betraying me. I could not physically drive my car due to chronic, acute pain. My fine motor skills and gross motor skills were severely impaired. I was told to go on a disability pension. I could have wallowed in self-pity but I didn't. Instead, I adapted and chose to use my brain. I started my education business called Educated Therapists, teaching and doing webinars and live training.

My reputation grew in the industry and I fast became known as an industry expert. That decision of refusing to accept the status quo and focusing on what I could do resulted in me breaking into the USA market with my brand.

Ask yourself when something happens that you don't expect. How do you respond to it? If it was not a reaction you were happy with, how would you like to respond in the future?

**Lesson Two - You are capable of far more than you give yourself credit for.**
The challenge with "realistic" goals is that they aren't inspiring. What is taught is goals to be "SMART". The acronym stands for Specific, Measurable, Achievable, Realistic and Timely. Every goal-setting exercise has said for your goals to be realistic.

Here is the challenge. When the shit hits the fan and you have never really pushed yourself outside of your boundaries, you don't believe you can pull off a miracle. You need to push the boundaries when things are going well, not attempt them when everything is falling apart. If you can't master your fear when things are good it will take over when things are going bad. The business owner who has mastered setting the goal extremely high and achieving it can weather the unpredictability of life and knows they are capable of much more.

COVID-19 was one of the most significant predictors of business success. How you coped with this unforeseen and unpredictable event tells you a lot about yourself. Did you do as I did and start finding alternative ways to earn income? Did you examine how you could do things differently? Did you go into the fetal position, paralysed with fear? How you responded will reveal a lot about your resilience. The thing is, resilience is a muscle and the more you develop it the better you become at handling those curve balls that business is going to throw at you.

**Lesson Three – Become like Teflon and let the hate slide off.**
There is one thing for sure: you will be judged and the haters will come. One of the hardest lessons I had to learn for resilience was to let the opinions of others just slide off me as if I was Teflon coated. I still felt the sting and hurt when I heard things but I got stronger and stronger in my own internal voice, so much so that it drowned out the opinions of others that were negative. If you allow the opinions of others to hurt you, you will not pick yourself back up when you need to. You will also not make the decisions you need to make for yourself or your business for "fear" of offending someone. You will become "trapped" in the opinion of others, effectively preventing yourself from becoming a leader.

The gossiping and rumours trickled back to me. I had comments mentioned to me, such as "I was money hungry and all I thought about was myself". Staff told me that some of the clinic owners said, "They wished someone else owned Roccoco". I was left wondering what on earth I had done to offend them, only to realise I had probably done nothing and that their opinion was based on hearsay and not actual interaction or knowledge of who I am. Everyone has an opinion on how things should be done. However, they cast their opinion without knowing all the facts surrounding any decision. They also cast their opinion based on how it affects them and it is filtered through their lens of the world. It isn't a big-picture perspective at all.

After my first spinal surgery I was left in chronic pain and unable to perform basic daily activities. The pain clinic I needed to attend was in Brisbane and there were no pain management facilities where I lived. I knew that I would forever struggle financially if I didn't get help. I wanted to relocate with my children but due to a parenting court order I had no choice but to go to court if I wanted to bring my children with me. I was only earning $44K in revenue then and the courts asked me to submit a business plan of my expected earnings over the next two years to prove I could support my children adequately. Ironically the figures I submitted were so made up and fantasy-like that I did not think I would achieve them and yet I ended up surpassing them.

During my court case psychologists interviewed my children. The psychologists report said they were both emotionally closer to me; in particular my oldest son Stuart was very close to me. I thought my determination and grit would be viewed favourably in the eyes of the court; it wasn't. My health status was used against me and I was told that they did not believe I would be able to care for my children properly, so the judge ruled that they were to remain with their father in Townsville. I couldn't believe it because he was unemployed.

I was utterly devastated by the decision. However, more of a concern for me was that my children wouldn't understand my decision and reasoning for going to Brisbane to manage my health. My biggest fear is that they would think I didn't love them. I carried that guilt around for years.

---

*"You will never be defeated by what others say about you. You will be defeated by what you say about YOU."*
**Bishop T.D. Jakes.**

---

The gossip started about me at the school with a lot of judgement from other women for my decision, some labelling me a "bad mother." Even when I relocated to Brisbane I received judgement from other mothers. How could any woman leave her children? They didn't understand at all. I had to let it slide off me for I knew it eats you up inside and devastates your self-esteem and worth.

## Lesson Four - Become the master

If you master not only your mind but your craft it is impossible for you not to succeed. Resilience requires you to be able to master change and adapt. After my first spinal surgery I was left in chronic pain for over eight years. For years my pain was, on average, a minimum of 5/10. It constantly interfered with my ability to function normally. 2017 was the year I started to become aware of what I was capable of, both physically and mentally. I had three surgeries in one year, bringing my count of major surgeries up to 4. It took a hard toll on my body which left me with a lot of healing to do. I told myself that if I could get through this I could achieve anything I desired if I put my mind to it. Even though I was in rehabilitation post-surgery and recovery for nine months, we still managed to double our revenue that year.

Success requires mastery of yourself. I realised that if I wanted to succeed I had to learn how to become the master of my mind - something that isn't the easiest thing to do when you don't have any health challenges. Chronic pain is even more difficult because it requires even more effort.

---

*"Master the topic, the message and the delivery."* **Steve Jobs**

---

Chronic pain is faulty signalling from the brain. It continues to signal that you are in danger when you aren't. The pain is "real", and you feel it. However, from a physiological perspective, your brain shouldn't be sending the message yet it continues to do so. I also learned that it takes time for neural pathways to stop and for new ones to grow. I read stories of inspiration from others who had managed to get rid of the pain through a continued focused effort. I figured if they could do it then so could I.

I delved into learning everything I could about pain and how the brain responds. I learnt that the brain processes pain and that the brain can be retrained; this is referred to as neuroplasticity. I was used to pushing myself before having had health issues. However, I soon learned that you couldn't "push" yourself to keep going when you have chronic pain. What happens with chronic pain is that if you push yourself, your ability to do tasks and activities becomes less and less each time you push too hard to the point that you can barely do anything.

It was a sobering reminder when I attended the Pain Clinic because, out of all attendees, I was the only one working. Everyone else was physically unable to work due to being incapacitated by pain. I thought to myself, "how can this be?" I was amazed that I was the only person still having a semblance of their past life before the pain. It shocked me that they had not learnt how to control pain and work with it rather than against it. The other patients were doing what the pain clinic referred to as "boom or bust". Instead of just cleaning one room of the house per day, they tried to do the whole house, which made their ability for activity keep lowering until they could barely do anything.

I learned first about neural networks of the brain from John Assaraf. It was from John's programs at NeuroGym that I learnt that the neural networks of the brain are plastic. This meant they could be moulded and reshaped. It was also around this time that I became exposed to the concept that our neural pathways also determine our results in life as patterns of behaviour keep us stuck in our current circumstances.

I explored the concept of binaural beats, which is a brain entrainment method, a direct way of hijacking your brainwaves to produce their own natural endorphins. I started listening to it daily and my pain improved so I could start working more. I started visualising my perfect health as it once had been. I created vision boards encompassing my business, health and personal life.

I also let go of guilt which was a shackle around my ankle. I had been letting other people's opinions of medications and their use influence my decisions. At the time I could only work about 5 hours a day and had to break it up into blocks of time. The pain made me incredibly fatigued. I couldn't attend anything during the day as I would sleep for 3 hours in the middle of the day. I hadn't been coping with the constant pain at all and my doctor had suggested going on an anti-depressant. I resisted initially as there is still so much stigma attached to anti-depressants. I had reached the point where I just wanted to function as normally as possible.

My pain went from a constant five down to a 1. It was incredible. I began focusing on growing my business again as I could focus better than ever. I knew I didn't want to stay on them forever but I was willing to swallow my pride for the moment to allow myself to cope better.

I was on anti-depressants for about three years. After my third spinal surgery I no longer required them as I had been walking around for three years with nerve compression down all four limbs of my body and the surgery had corrected it. Letting go of the opinions of others is liberating. Only you can decide what is best for you.

Resilience is not something that is obtained through ease. It is the ability to recover psychologically from obstacles, trauma and significant stress levels. Resilience can only be obtained from hardship and not when everything goes to plan. Resilience is obtained through overwhelming difficulty, falling repeatedly and each time getting back up again and starting afresh. In a world of instant satisfaction, resilience is a dying trait that is necessary not only for business success but also in life. Without resilience and the ability to adapt psychologically we can succumb to mental illnesses like depression. Resilience is a set of behaviours and thinking that allow you to adapt and move through crises in life. Resilience is not only essential for business success but to adapt to the challenges life can throw at us.

# CHAPTER FOUR

## How To Grow Your Business 400% — Without Working Longer Hours —

# CHAPTER FOUR

## How To Grow Your Business 400%
## — Without Working Longer Hours —

One of my considerable breakthroughs in business came when I discovered Pareto's principle. Italian economist Vilfredo Pareto developed the principle. The rule states that 20% of your efforts produce 80% of your results. It also means that 80% of your revenue comes from 20% of your clients. After discovering this I realised that if I got more of the 20% of clients generating lots of income, I would grow my business by 400% without working one hour more. The 20% of clients who gave me a lot of revenue also required less work to manage.

Pareto's Principle can help us identify the most essential tasks that need to be completed to accomplish our goals and identify the perfect customer that will exponentially grow your business. It shows you where to focus your time to leverage the activities that give you the highest return for your energy investment.

We have seen this directly in our own business which is how I grew our revenue by 500% and dropped the number of clinics we had by 60%. About four years ago we had over 550 clinics. We changed our terms of trade and started focusing on whom we wanted as a customer. We dropped 350 clinics, and as a result, we only dealt with our ideal client. Our revenue grew 500%. We focused our marketing on our ideal customers and started attracting these clinics. They took less work and spent more money, resulting in a more profitable business.

For Pareto's principle to work you need to identify which 20% of your efforts are producing 80% of your results (potentially, more importantly, which 80% aren't working for you). The best way to identify those efforts is to dive deeply into how you spend your time.   Doing a time audit can help you get a clear picture of how you spend your time daily—and, more importantly, which of your daily tasks produce results.

---

*"If you're interested, you will do what is convenient.*
*If you're committed, you'll do whatever it takes."*
**John Assaraf.**

---

A time audit can seem like a waste of time.  I felt like that initially as I had numerous business coaches ask me to do this as part of their advice.  I resisted it massively.  Detail is not my greatest strength and this task required me to be very detailed.  Previously I had found it to be a painful exercise ... so, for ages, I resisted.  I never did one until my coach pitched me on what I would benefit by doing one.  She sold me on the process by explaining that by doing it I would be able to reach the next level of business and achieve everything I wanted, so I committed to doing one.  After I performed the time audit I realised I wasn't managing my day.  I had continual interruptions that broke my concentration, resulting in wasted time and loss of productivity.

A University of California study found that refocusing after each interruption takes over 23 minutes.  So constant interruptions result in a massive loss of productivity.  Another study found that if the interruption takes you onto another task, multitasking saps your brain power. The result is that you don't have the attention or energy for critical decision-making.

After I started blocking out my time and setting rules around when staff could come and speak to me, my productivity skyrocketed. I was no longer distracted; there were scheduled times each day when they could come and get help.

*So, how do you do a time audit?*
For one week, track how you spend every minute of your day, both in and out of work. I use an excel spreadsheet to track time and do an audit or you can just keep track using a pen and notebook. It's not important how you track your time. What's important is that you track where every minute is going.

Did you spend 10 minutes in between meetings scrolling through Facebook? Log it. Did you spend your entire morning on client calls? Log it, including the detail of whom you spoke to, so you can track your interactions with clients and an increase in revenue. Did you spend time trawling through your inbox? Log it, log it, log it.

After a whole week of tracking your time you'll have an accurate outline of where your time is going and once you have that it becomes much easier to identify what is time well spent (20%)—and what is time wasted (80%).

The important thing to also note is that no day is the same for most entrepreneurs. I never had a day that was the same and that had always been my excuse for not doing a time audit. I would say to my coach, "But it wasn't a normal week," and my coach would say, "You never have a normal week Jacine." It was then that I realised she was right. I don't ever have a typical week. So, I started tracking it because time is your most precious commodity.

### *The First Mistake*

The first mistake that business owners make is focusing on the wrong tasks. They spend too much time on tasks that don't generate income and not enough time on tasks that do. Whilst it is essential for administration and other business tasks, it is better to outsource these and focus on the activities that generate income for the business. When you have deadlines and staff asking for help it can be easy to pacify the one who screams the loudest. However, you really need to sit back and ask yourself this one question:

"Is this taking me towards my goals and growing my revenue?"

Often it is administrative tasks that need to be done, but it isn't the activity that will move the money needle the quickest. As a business owner it can be easy to distract yourself with emails, tasks and other activities because it makes you feel like you have "achieved" something. However, the measurement you need to look at is not your task list; it should be your revenue and profit. Your task list is never going to be empty. It is delusional to think it will be. Set yourself up to succeed instead of fail.

Too many businesses go through a rollercoaster of revenue with some months being good and others being terrible. They spend time bringing in new leads only to drop their marketing to fulfil this work. There isn't a strategy for their marketing funnel to be continuously filled and they haven't employed anyone to deal with this. Instead they spend their time on it instead of outsourcing.

One of the biggest mistakes business owners make is trying to do EVERYTHING. You strangle a business when you don't let go of control and allow others to step in so that you can do what you excel at. I also see business owners not focusing enough on income-producing activities. They may spend too much energy looking for new ways to generate income but don't do anything with what they have, which can lead to financial problems down the line. I often see owners asking how they can bring in more customers but they have no clear marketing plan for the existing customers. It is a known fact that getting more money out of existing clients is easier than finding a new one, yet this is often overlooked in business growth.

We have had periods in our business when we have been sliding backwards with revenue and my first instinct is to see where we are dropping in revenue so we know where we need to focus. I have never looked for more clients when a financial crisis occurs. I work with what I have because if it drops, something has been missed. Something with the service or communication has not been optimal and revenue improves whenever we have done this. Only after this do we start looking for other sources of income. Keep your existing customers happy and look after them because they are gold.

Before going out and looking for new customers, examine your business and ask yourself what you could do that you are not already doing. Make a list of marketing activities that you could be doing. Below are just a few of them:

1. Regular newsletters – email direct response marketing is one of the most effective ways to market to a customer base that is already engaged. Yet, it is one of the most underutilised

marketing methods. We also were guilty of not utilising our email list in business. However, we learned how much money can be generated using it effectively.

I am often surprised by how often many business owners do not have an email list for their business. They don't collect data such as birthdays which could be used for promotions for special occasions. Even worse is the business owner who has an email list but doesn't do anything with it, so their customers rarely hear from them. An email list also aids if you choose to sell your business at a later stage.

Businesses often don't utilise newsletters because they often wonder what on earth they would write about. Newsletters should have some reason for communicating with your customers. It could be as simple as highlighting a new service or product, introducing a new team member or promoting your special, educating them on something you do or sell, tips and hints on getting the best out of your service or product. You want to give them a reason to open your email consistently, or at least not delete them.

2. Consistently posting on social media – many businesses post and then don't post for weeks. The way the algorithms work is that when you follow this pattern, even if someone has liked your page, you no longer show up in their newsfeed.

When we first started on Instagram it was a new platform and we had to set reminders to post on our phones or we would forget. We looked at the insights and found that, with our audience, the best time to post was 11 am, so we set the alarm on our phone for a month to remind us to post.  Habits take time to form, but this is how you post regularly.

Posts can now also be prescheduled and planned out.  I always suggest businesses spend 20 minutes maximum on a post.  Suppose you post four times a week; that is only 16 posts for a month.  You should be able to spend 6 hours maximum doing your posts, and they are then done for the entire month.  If you don't have time, outsource to a virtual assistant who can do this for you.  Many artificial intelligence apps can assist you with writing social media posts.  Your virtual assistant doesn't necessarily need to be knowledgeable about your business.  You just need to approve them, and they can schedule the posts.  Apps such as Rytr and Jasper allow anyone to copywrite without experience.

We have grown our brand through social media and it is the cheapest advertising you will ever have because it only costs your time.  You have access to millions of potential customers for free, yet when I talk about social media to most business owners they groan and tell me they don't like it.  Yet the same businesses also are not doing any paid advertising and wonder why their businesses struggle.

3.  Following up on your customers.  Most businesses never follow up with their customers at all.  The reality is that most customers won't tell you when they are unhappy.  They just go somewhere else.  I have seen this in the esthetics industry where a customer is sold a product and the therapist doesn't hear about it till the next time they go to the salon.  If you are introducing a new product to a client, follow them up to ensure there are no issues with use and to ensure they have understood how to use it.

In most instances, any adverse events or complications can be resolved quickly after purchase. When there is no follow-up, many lose business simply because they did not check to ensure everything was satisfactory. There is an expression that says, "The way someone treats you after the sale shows their true intent". This means that if you genuinely want a customer for life you will express concern and ensure your customers are happy. If you just want a sale then there is no aftersales follow-up.

4. Contact past customers about updating their website or their photos. My company, Roccoco, has been in business for ten years and had seven websites. None of the previous suppliers I dealt with ever contacted me again after my initial purchase to offer a refreshed website. They also never kept in contact with me so they drifted off my radar and I forgot about them. The person who remains in touch is the first person they think of when they need a similar service again.

We send out charity greeting cards every year to our customers for Christmas. Every single one is handwritten. The company we buy the cards from every year reaches out to us to offer us a complimentary 10-pack because they know we buy thousands yearly. It is because they continue to reach out that they get our business.

If you are a restaurant or a service business then you can utilise wedding anniversaries, birthdays and special occasions to attract your customers back into your business. When we bought our BMW, the salesperson asked what I also drove and if it was leased. He was an intelligent salesperson. He knew when my lease was due to expire and he also knew I was likely to purchase, so he contacted me before my lease ran out so that I was thinking about him when the time came that I was ready to swap out my vehicle.

Stay in touch with your customers regularly. This has never ceased to amaze me that suppliers don't contact me via phone or book an appointment to see me. I have told every supplier I have dealt with in the industry from the first meeting that the person who speaks to me the most gets the most money. It is my way of telling them if they want to do well with our company they need to communicate with me regularly. There are many suppliers we deal with. The ones who are very active and make an effort to see me are the ones who get our spending dollars for product development.

It isn't rocket science. It is simple. When I want to formulate something new, they are the first person I ask to see what actives are available. They are at the top of my mind. The business that gets the most orders out of our company also contacts me just to say hello, for no other reason. Not every call is a sales pitch. This builds rapport and a strong relationship with this company.

## The Second Mistake

The second mistake is not focusing on the right customers. Many business owners focus on a customer demographic that doesn't provide them with an opportunity to make money. I often see this within industries that are "spiritual or helping others". These business owners continue to struggle because the customers they are trying to help simply can't afford their services. These are the carers and the nurturers, and because they generally are not good at setting up boundaries, customers often take advantage of them. The same businesses usually also don't charge enough even to be profitable. They don't value themselves enough and consequently they undercharge. For many of them, they remain unprofitable. The reality is that people don't truly value or appreciate free things. I have been given free courses but I have never done one of them. I made sure I devoted the time to the ones I paid for.

My first business failed because I was not charging enough and I couldn't determine why I was making no money. At the time I had an extreme poverty mindset. I believed that anybody charging over $100 for a skincare product was ripping people off. As much as I am now horrified at how I thought, that was what I believed at that time. All it did was show my naivety with business. I had no understanding of needing to price for distributors and wholesalers. I didn't think about the cost of advertising or the running costs of a business. I didn't think about liability insurance, and because I didn't consider these things, my first brand, Eclogite, failed.

I have seen this within the esthetics industry where many clinicians discount their treatments and give away free products because they genuinely want to help. Most of them don't realise that their customers often can afford it but won't prioritise it. I had been guilty of this 20 years ago. I was giving away products and discounting, thinking my customers "couldn't afford it". When I discovered my client was going on an overseas holiday I initially felt angry. At that time in my life, I couldn't even afford to go on a holiday, yet my client was doing the one thing I couldn't do. It was a big learning lesson for me. I learned not to judge the client and that clients have more money than they let on. I also learnt that they would find the money if it were enough of a priority. I stopped discounting after that.

Just because you could do something in business doesn't mean you SHOULD do it. The first rule of business is that there must be a demand for your service or product. The second rule is that people need to be willing to pay an amount that will allow you to make a healthy profit and run a viable business. If you can't abide by the second rule, don't start a business out of the service or product. It will fail.

A lack of market research or not understanding the market's needs can lead to a business failure. Maintaining a healthy relationship with customers is crucial for any company. This is especially true in the digital age where customers can access all sorts of information, forcing companies to be transparent about their products, services and policies.

**The Third Mistake**

The third mistake they make is thinking that everybody is their customer. So, they try to be everything to everybody and instead become invisible to most customers. With no clear marketing message or differentiation, it becomes impossible for them to stand out; just like "Where's Wally", they blend in with their competition and end up competing on price.

Until the value is shown to the customer, they have no CHOICE but to look at the price. Whenever I have asked a business owner to identify what makes them unique, they are unable to do so. They struggle with articulating what makes them unique and different. As I say to my coaching clients, "If you as the business owner can't tell me what makes you unique, then how on earth is your customer going to know?" The business owner knows their business in much more detail, yet many cannot identify why they are different.

If you can't sell and you are in business, you need to learn quickly or don't go into business unless you can employ someone who can sell. Copywriting is salesmanship in print and it is crucial for a business owner to either learn or outsource it. The challenge is that finding a decent copywriter is now incredibly difficult, which is why learning it yourself is a skill that has enormous value. There are many copywriters to claim to be able to be experts at the skill, but many are overpriced and do not deliver. When looking at a sales page, ask the question, "Would this convince me to buy this product?" because good copywriting should.

The most important thing you can do for your business's success is to sit down and identify what makes your business unique. Examine what your competitors do and then write down how you do it differently. Is it a process you do differently? Do you make a guarantee where others don't? Is your product superior? Are your products multifunctional?

Identify who your dream buyer is and focus relentlessly on them. There are two reasons for this. The first is that it brings clarity to your marketing message. The second is that it activates your brain's RAS or reticular activating system. The reticular activating system is a part of the brain that filters incoming stimuli. This means that it helps us to concentrate on what we want to pay attention to and filter out everything else.

Have you ever driven past a store but never noticed it because you didn't need what they sold at the time? Your brain is filtering out information that isn't important to you. When you prime the brain to what it is you desire, it will take notice and see everything that will take you towards that goal.

## Focus On Key Clients

As mentioned in the earlier example, a small percentage of your clients and customers are often responsible for a considerable percentage of your revenue. So, if you want to drive more revenue and take your business to the next level, you need to identify and stick with those clients or customers.

Take a deep dive into your finances. Identify where most of your revenue is coming from. Narrow down your client or customer list so you're focusing your time and efforts on the people bringing the majority of your revenue in.  Not only will this make your business easier to manage, but it's likely to increase revenue. You're much more likely to drive revenue by providing a higher level of service to clients and customers who are already spending money than by spinning your wheels with the other 80%, that aren't contributing to your bottom line in a significant way.

Focus on your top 20% of customers.
Focus on your top 20% of products.
Focus on the top 20% of sales channels.
Focus on the top 20% of geographical locations that are bringing money in.
Focus on removing the 80% that is not generating effectively.

Every year we analyse our top-performing products and examine whether to keep the poor performers or reformulate them and improve them.

So, the Pareto principle says that 20% of your efforts produce 80% of your results. But the flip side of that can also be true!  If something in your business is taking up 80% of your time, energy or resources but is only producing 20% of your results (like a difficult client), get rid of it! That is what we have done. We removed the clients who were consuming our time and barely purchasing anything.

Once you focus on your dream customer and can identify who they are and their traits, it makes it much easier to identify not only who your customer is but also what they want. This is crucial because it allows you to bypass their logical brain and go straight to their emotions. As we mentioned previously, as much as we like to think we are logical, we are not. As humans, we are emotional creatures, and we buy with our emotions, so tapping into emotions is literally tapping into their wallets.

If you look at the photo below and I don't tell you what you should be trying to find, how will you see a cat?

Going through and identifying what you are looking for makes it easier to recognise it when it appears. This has amazed me not only in business but also in dating. So many people have no clue what they are looking for and they go for the first thing that comes along. It often ends in disaster and then they say dating or business doesn't work.

## Psychographics Is More Critical Than Demographics.

If you have ever wondered why customers do what they do, then you are exploring psychographics. Psychographics is the study of personality and individual differences. It is a way to categorise people into different groups based on their attitudes, interests, opinions and lifestyle choices. Psychographic marketing is a technique that uses psychographic profiles to identify groups of people with similar characteristics.

Psychographic marketing aims to target the right customers with messages that will resonate with them. It can be used for branding awareness or product positioning. Psychographic profiles are built using data from surveys, questionnaires and interviews. The data collected can include demographic information and their attitudes, interests, opinions and lifestyle choices. Data from social media platforms such as Facebook also provides insights into what matters to people in different age groups or geographical locations. Psychographics reveals what motivates your customer to buy your service or product. It reveals why they buy one product over another. It also reveals their reason for purchasing.

There may be numerous reasons why a customer purchases a luxury vehicle in the luxury car industry. For some customers, their focus will be on features and comfort. Other purchasers will buy a luxury vehicle as a status symbol of their success. If a customer is purchasing anything other than a basic model of an item, then psychographics is at play. Once you understand what it is that is motivating them you can directly tap into their psychology.

Psychographic profiling is very effective because consumers often make decisions based on psychographic aspects such as personal preferences and values. By understanding the psychological characteristics of your audience you can significantly improve your reach methods and advertising styles and create an emotionally engaging brand overall.

In our experience, there may be people you perceive would not purchase your product as they don't fit the demographic profile. The customer may not have a high income. If you used demographics only, you might exclude this customer. However, if the psychographic profile is right and the product or service you are selling fills a huge pain point, then demographics become irrelevant. The customer will find the money.

**Prince Charles**

- Male
- Born in 1948
- Raised in the UK
- Married twice
- Lives in a castle
- Wealthy & famous

**Ozzy Osbourne**

- Male
- Born in 1948
- Raised in the UK
- Married twice
- Lives in a castle
- Wealthy & famous

✳ Personas shouldn't be about demographics. Personas should be about the problems & challenges people face.

Since the term was first coined in 1971, the marketing world has used psychographics to understand consumers better and identify their most attractive interests. This type of marketing aims to increase sales by knowing what kind of product or service consumers are most likely to purchase. Psychographic segmentation divides customers into groups based on their lifestyles, interests, values and attitudes. This type of segmentation is often used for targeting products or services, so it's essential for those involved in marketing.

Cognitive Psychographics or, as it's sometimes referred to in the business world, "mindset", looks at how people think and process information, their likes and dislikes and beliefs. This can include things like your level of optimism or pessimism, how much control you believe you have over your life and whether you prefer structure or freedom.

The reasons why your customer buys are far more critical. Once you understand what the psychographics of your customers are, you can utilise this to engage emotional triggers that pull them into your brand and resonate with them. Knowing who your ideal customer is allows you to tap into their fears, dreams and feelings. As previously stated, humans are emotional creatures, not logical. We justify our purchasing decisions logically, but the decision was made emotionally. When you understand their biggest fears and frustrations you can effortlessly market to them ethically because you are solving their problem.

Ask your customers why they buy your products. What is their pain point or most significant benefit from using your product or service? Once you tap into the hidden reason they purchase you can leverage this with your marketing.

## How Do You Identify Who Your Ideal Customer Is?

The first step is to write down a list of whom you would like to do business with. What are their personality traits? How does interacting with them make you feel? Do you feel inspired by interacting with them? The simple act of writing down the character traits attracts the ideal type of customer to you. My coach got me to write a list of traits of my perfect customer. She asked me to write a list of 100 things about them. When you first start to write it you will come up with demographics such as they are married, they earn so much income. After you run out of logical-brained information, your subconscious will be forced to delve deeper, and this is where you find the psychographic information.

It is imperative to do this because you may have customers who fit the psychographic profile of an ideal customer. Still, they are challenging to deal with, cause issues and are downright stressful. There have been numerous times when I have experienced this in business. Over the past eleven years we have fired just under ten customers. The level of stress that came from them was not worth any money they gave me.

After doing this activity, review your current customers and analyse who gives you the most money. Examine if these top 20% of customers have anything in common. We interviewed ours to find out why they chose our brand. It gave us much valuable information to utilize for our future marketing.

I have done this several times in our business. You can imagine my frustration when I realised that some of our top customers were anything but enjoyable to work with. It wasn't just me who felt like this. They were also stressing out my team. They were entitled, demanding and draining not only for me but also for my team. We refocused our list to the customers we wanted and we started attracting clinics more aligned with us. We did not need to fire the remaining clinics that were not in alignment. They just naturally drifted away as they were not in resonance with us.

If your top customers are not whom you want, examine your marketing. Are you putting out an incongruent message? Have you set clear expectations of your requirements for doing business with you? If not, then implement something. People treat you how you allow them to treat them.

## Embrace Automation

When you finish your time inventory and examine how you're spending your time, chances are you're going to identify some tasks that you can't eliminate and aren't producing results. For those tasks, the best thing you can do is to embrace automation. Automation is a great way to streamline tasks in your business that are necessary but aren't necessarily producing many results. Within most companies, customer service is a repetition of the same information. By templating responses you can save a lot of repetition and time. It makes your business and team far more productive.

As we started growing, we discovered we were spending a lot of time rewriting the same content over and over. This was when I decided to start automating some of our emails. We made a list of the most frequently asked questions and wrote templates for all of them. We templated the information about our products, how to use them and why they were beneficial for the skin. This saved hours and hours. Initially, we looked for free software as we had a limited budget at the time. We chose HubSpot for this as there was a free option. We eventually moved onto a paid version, and as we grew, we changed to another software to accommodate the needs of the business.

You can automate your social media with pre-scheduling apps which allows you to focus on doing all your posts in one session for the month. There are many apps such as Planoly and Hootsuite. Facebook also has the option to plan your posts and schedule them to go live outside of working hours. You can do this through the Business Manager.

## Customer Loyalty And Retention

The best customer is one that is not just loyal to your product but also gives back as well. They are the ones who will recommend your products to their friends and family. The key to finding an ideal customer is understanding what motivates them, what they need and how they like to communicate.

Some customers simply want to buy something to use as an impulse purchase. Other customers might be loyal because they believe in your company's mission and believe it is going to be successful in the near future. Customer loyalty also comes from the functionality of your product and the value of the experience that you provide them with.

Customer loyalty is a critical component in the success of any business. Companies must create a strategy for customer loyalty and prioritise it. This can be done by implementing customer-focused marketing strategies, providing excellent customer service and giving customers incentives to return.

There are many ways that companies can promote customer loyalty, but there are three main areas that should be considered: customer-focused marketing strategies, excellent customer service and incentives for returning customers.

## Customer-Focused Marketing Strategies

Customer-focused marketing strategies include a variety of ways to reach consumers with direct messages, including direct mail, email marketing and social media marketing.

## Ask Their Opinion

One of the ways to make customers feel valued it to ask their opinion. When I have done product development there have been times where I did surveys and polls to ask the opinion of our customers. We used this knowledge in our product development. It makes the customer feel important and special, but also gave us valuable insight into what they were looking for in a product as well.

## Engage Your Customers

The more customers engage with you, the more loyalty you will command from them. If you only connect with customers when you want a sale, they won't stay for long. You can engage customers by giving them gifts that are branded to your company. It keeps you top of mind when they are purchasing.

## Direct Mail

Direct mail marketing is one of the most influential and cost-effective marketing methods. It is a powerful tool for companies looking to promote their products or services. The idea behind direct mail marketing is that it provides customers with a tangible experience, increasing their chances of purchasing your product or service.

Various types of businesses can use direct mail marketing, which can be tailored to suit each business's needs.

## Email Marketing

Email marketing allows companies to reach customers with timely, personalised messages tailored to their needs. It also provides a way for marketers to measure the success of their campaigns as well as deliver highly targeted offers.

Some marketers think email is dead, but this is not true. It is an easy way to market to your customers. Just ensure your emails serve a purpose and add value. Your emails should be a mixture of sales pitches and valuable information. You can use email to educate your customers on new offers. These are called awareness campaigns.

Email sequencing is the foundation of sales funnels. Sales funnels aim to lead your customers through a journey until they are ready to purchase from your company. The reality is that only 3% of customers are ready to purchase right this minute. So, the 3% of your target audience ready to buy right away can simply respond to one of your ads. If the desire to solve their problem is strong enough and your ad appears in front of them at the right time, you may be lucky to close the sale.

A further 6-7% of people are willing to purchase. However, if the price point is higher, they will need significant convincing through either an irresistible offer or a guarantee. Another 30% don't realise they have an issue and another 30% are not interested based on the current information they have.

Emails are one of the quickest and cheapest ways to stay relevant to your audience and to update them with the latest news and offerings.

## Social Media Marketing

We grew our brand, Roccoco Botanicals, entirely through social media. The year we decided to open an Instagram account we doubled our revenue. That is the power of social media. There are over 15 social media platforms you could possibly use. However, it doesn't mean that all are appropriate or that you should use all of them. We primarily use Facebook, Instagram, YouTube, Google My Business and TikTok.

The top platforms that exist for social media are:
1.   Facebook
2.   Instagram
3.   Tik Tok
4.   YouTube
5.   Pinterest
6.   LinkedIn
7.   Google My Business
8.   Twitch
9.   WhatsApp
10.  Snapchat
11.  Yelp
12.  Tumblr
13.  WeChat
14.  BeReal

Facebook has the biggest audience with nearly 3 billion active monthly users. Facebook is our primary way of doing business with older users aged 35 plus. If you look at social sites, they will say that Facebook is primarily used by 18-30-year-old customers. However, that is not our experience. We find a lot of older clients are on Facebook and very active. It is my primary way of doing B2B and attracting clinics. I also have Facebook Groups that I utilise to drive business for B2B and B2C. It allows us to engage in a way with our customers that Instagram does not permit. The searchability of groups is a bonus because new customers can search for previous threads.

Instagram has over 2 billion users. Fashion, beauty or health and fitness tend to do well on Instagram. Instagram is designed for visually appealing merchandise. Instagram also taps into the influencer market, giving brands and businesses another way to get their message out.

Instagram also has shopping on the platform. We often have customers message us on Instagram, making it a valuable tool to talk directly to customers to address their questions and help them select the appropriate product. Instagram blew up our business in just 12 months.

---

*"Just as you don't need to be on every single TV channel, I don't believe a brand needs to be on every single social media one in a big way."* **Shiv Singh**

---

YouTube is also popular with influencers. If you want to reach and engage with your audience on the platform but also with a google search, then YouTube is perfect. YouTube is the platform where people spend the most time. My children don't watch TV; they watch YouTube. It is also an untapped market for marketers because most brands are not using it.

Google My Business is an essential platform because most consumers check Google Reviews before dealing with a business. This platform is one of the most underutilised platforms for marketing. Most people don't update any information on their Google profile, leaving money on the table. If you have a physical business, use Google Business Profile to your advantage.

Google My Business allows you to get discovered in Google Maps. This also improves your Search Engine Optimisation (SEO) and you are more likely to appear when people search for other businesses in the same proximity.

You can post updates on Google My Business. This creates solid local SEO, and this will rank in searches. It will rank above any other third-party services.

TikTok appeals to a younger generation, but it can't be ignored. If you want to stay relevant to up-and-coming generations you should use it. TikTok has over one billion users. Users spend over an hour on the platform. It is an excellent platform for beauty and personal care, clothing, coaching, travel and food.

The most important thing to do with any social media platform is to monitor and record your data. If you are not analysing, then you can't compare. Numbers allow you to determine your growth and impact. If you are not tracking them you can't get an accurate picture of whether your actions are making an impact.

**Excellent Customer Service**
It seems just too obvious, doesn't it? The lack of customer service is appalling. It isn't hard to succeed. Just give excellent customer

service and they will come back because your competitors often are not giving any customer service. They make doing business with them difficult and frustrating. There have been businesses I have dealt with that treated me incredibly poorly. I was so surprised at the way things had been handled. Not only was I poorly treated, they also never apologised. Therefore, not only will I never do business with them, I will tell the whole world about them so others don't have the same experience.

## Incentives For Returning Customers

It is easier to keep an existing customer and sell more to them than to get a new one. Customer loyalty programs can keep your customers coming back to you. Therefore, you need to have a retention strategy to ensure you keep bringing your clients back to you.

Incentives for returning customers might be discounts or special deals offered to people who return frequently or discounts on a new product for those who return after trying it.

It is naïve if you think your customers will not shop elsewhere if the product is cheaper. If your customers shop online, ask, "Why are they doing it?" Is it because the product is cheaper online? If so, have you told your customers you will price match? If they buy online you have lost the sale anyway; it is better to get some money than no money. I have stubbornly seen business owners who outright refuse to do this. They believe they shouldn't have to, so they lose the sale. Most of these businesses also don't have any loyalty system.

Ask yourself whether they are buying online for convenience. Many businesses do not have a website and customers may find it difficult to purchase products. Other businesses don't have staff and make the customer book a time to pick up the product. It just becomes too hard for the customer and it is easier for them to shop online. Convenience is King. This is why convenience stores exist. They charge an exorbitant price for the convenience of obtaining a product quickly and out of hours and their customers are happy to pay for the privilege of getting the item they need.

Do you have a rewards system for your customers? Coffee franchises and nail bars were the first to implement this. On your sixth visit you got a discount. Do you do the same? Now I hear some of you screaming, "But I shouldn't have to!!!" You certainly don't have to, but remember that the customer can choose whom they go to. You don't own your customers; if they can save money, they will. There is no apparent difference for many businesses, so consumers have a choice.

If you are a business owner then you need to acknowledge that it is a competitive environment. There is no point complaining about how your customer shops if you are unwilling to change how you do business. Many business owners stubbornly stamp their feet and refuse to be flexible with how they do business. It is easier to acknowledge that customer loyalty is rare and to recognise that you must cultivate loyalty to ensure you get the maximum time out of a customer. Rewards systems, convenience and personal touches by the business are ways to retain customer loyalty.

Many business owners, particularly in the beauty industry, believe their customer owes them something. It is an entitlement culture that many business owners possess. They give too much away for free and when the customer purchases elsewhere, the business owner becomes resentful, not towards the customer but towards the company they are buying from. Could you imagine Harvey Norman getting angry at Apple because Apple did a different promotion? Instead, their customers would remain with them if they focused on building a loyalty program. If businesses made it easy for the customer to buy from them and they price match, customers would never leave. There are very few clinics that do this. Some of you are already saying that I am just a small business and can't afford to discount and price match. I am telling you that you can't afford not to.

## Become The Expert

If you do not advertise your business via paid methods, you will need to become an expert in your area of operation. We grew our brand by positioning ourselves as the expert. Many of the new experts are students I initially taught. One student stated that she had learnt everything about acne from me.

So how do you become an expert? Continued learning. It is said that less than 5% of people ever rise to the top. Mastery requires complete devotion to a topic to become good at it. It is quoted that more than 10,000 hours are required. However, in this ever-changing environment and with research being updated each year, it has never been more critical to keep up to date.

Marketing is a classic example. Every year the parameters and criteria change. What was allowed one year for advertising is now not allowed. The one thing that doesn't change is human psychology. So become a master of understanding this and you will always be able to reach your audience.

Whatever your area of business, it is critical for you to be educating your customers. This is the only way you get yourself out there as an expert. What you share must be new, original, unheard of and something that grabs their attention. You won't make an impact if you just regurgitate the same information as everyone else. When I started my business I started sharing information that conflicted with other professionals. It got people's attention. I didn't mean to be deliberately antagonistic. Everything that I said, I had research journal studies to validate what I was saying. It positioned me very quickly as an expert and I got a large following which is how I broke into the USA market.

**How Can You Position Yourself As An Expert?**

1. Be Consistent. You will never gain expert status if you don't post regularly or consistently. This is critical for gaining traction. When I first started I was consistently doing webinars and writing articles. I was highly active in groups on Facebook and regularly showcased my expertise. Create a consistent tone of communication on your website, blog and social media posts.

2. Be visible. You may be the absolute expert on a subject, but unless you're communicating your knowledge to others, you'll never be able to build a reputation as an expert. Online forums, social media and publications are buzzing with conversations about any and every topic. The more you can confidently dive in and make helpful, valuable contributions to relevant discussions, the more you'll be able to build a following for your brand. This is exactly how we grew our reputation.

   Your consistency will attract the interest of other people in the industry, including authority figures that matter in your industry. This is how I ended up writing for a professional journal. I was invited to do so. You can reach out to people and ask them to speak at their events. Business networking events are always looking for speakers. Many publications online are also looking for content for articles. One such place is SourceBottle. This is where you can submit articles that they are requesting.

Speak on a podcast. There are so many podcasts now that you could potentially talk on. Join business networking forums and socialize on them and build relationships. Through this relationship-building you will be invited to speak on podcasts. I have been invited to speak on numerous podcasts by attending networking functions and awards ceremonies. You also don't have to have a multimillion-dollar business either; just showcase your area of expertise consistently and you will naturally attract people to you.

3. Choose a niche and make it yours. Identify your area of interest and learn everything you can about it. You will naturally rise to the top. Having lots of information about many things is great, but it makes you a generalist. When you are unwell, you go to a specialist. They are experts in a small area. You need to do the same in your business. Some argue against niching. I disagree. Whenever I have seen this argument come up with niching, it is someone who isn't doing over a million dollars in revenue. Those who do niche own their niche, and they are the ultimate experts, which is why they earn millions.

4. Keep studying and learning. Many industries are constantly changing. To be a master you must continue to learn. Once qualified, many people no longer keep up to date with the latest developments. I remember going to a chemist's conference, and the presentation was on colourless turmeric. I was amazed that there were chemists present who were completely oblivious to this ingredient and they were so excited. This ingredient had

been out for over 15 years. We had been using it since the inception of our brand 11 years ago. Yet for these chemists it was news. Your ability to keep up to date will also shine through because you will be the leader and innovator.

## No And Low-Cost Ways Of Marketing

- Emails. Some marketers will tell you that email is dead. It isn't. It is one of the quickest ways to get a sale.

- Letterbox drops. Another marketing tactic that people will tell you doesn't work. I did this for my first business, acquiring ten customers out of one street. I also did it just two years ago for my skin clinic, and it brought in new customers. When I opened the clinic, we had zero customers. We didn't have a list and this strategy worked. If you have an irresistible offer it will get them through your door. The chances are that if you do a fantastic job you will retain them.

- Ask your clients for testimonials and use them to your advantage. If you don't ask for them, you rarely ever get them. Make sure you don't bribe people for them though. Use these testimonials on your website, blog and social media.

- Do joint ventures with other people. Find someone whose audience is similar but you are selling complementary products. Examples could include a gym partnering with a supplement company.

- Utilise video. There are so many options now for video content and video will outperform text every time. Post videos on YouTube using keywords that are relevant to your niche. This allows your videos to be ranked and found.

- Blogs. Blogs are one of the most incredible ways to deliver content that Google ranks and customers find value with. Often business owners don't write blogs because they over-analyse. If you come from a technical background, just remember that most customers don't understand technical jargon. Keep it simple and something the client will easily understand.

- Entice new customers and maintain high customer satisfaction; some businesses offer a trial period where you can try their product or service before committing to a purchase.

# CHAPTER FIVE

— Releasing The Shackles —

# CHAPTER FIVE

## —— Releasing The Shackles ——

The one thing that will hold you back in business is how you think. As Henry Ford said, "Whether you think you can or think you can't, either way you are right." How we think is nothing more than the sum of our environment, parenting and beliefs instilled when we were children.

Four things can hold you back. The first is the way you were raised. The second is letting the opinions of others influence you. The third is media, and the fourth is your peer group.

The beliefs of your parents and the environment you grew up in have a massive influence on your current belief systems surrounding money and your capabilities. If you grew up thinking money was scarce, that would become your belief about money. The way we think comes from the programming in our childhood before age seven unless we intentionally act to change it.

The opinions of others are another massive impactor on your progress. Many people lack a strong identity of themselves and so are easily influenced by the views of others. If other people tell you it isn't possible, you may buy into that story they are telling, and it will prevent you from taking the necessary risks you need to grow your business.

The programming we have. The media specifically will put you into a state of fear. Their job is not to tell you the news but to program you into a particular way of thinking. Mainstream media does not allow you to think positively. If you are watching it, then you will never attract the life you want. It is impossible. There is a reason they call them programs on TV; they are programming you!

But Jacine, I need to be informed!! Actually, no you don't. I haven't watched the news for over 25 years. If something really urgent is happening, somebody tells me about it. I remember when cyclone Yasi was coming in North Queensland. I had no idea until someone told me. I still had plenty of time to be prepared, and I didn't have to feed off the fear and hysteria that filled others. The same happened when restrictions came into force for COVID. It was others who were telling me what the restrictions were.

Your subconscious mind is easily programmed. TV does it effortlessly. The challenge is that whilst we may consciously attempt to achieve something, we can't activate our conscious mind all the time. It would be exhausting. Instead, our subconscious is what is truly driving our results and it is in charge almost 95% of the time. Willpower is using the conscious mind. It only lasts for so long. Without changing the subconscious mind you are fighting an uphill battle. Until they are both heading in the same direction you will experience things such as procrastination.

Procrastination is a classic sign of incongruency between your conscious and subconscious mind. Your subconscious and conscious mind are going in opposite directions, which is why you don't gain traction with your business. I learnt this when I initially tried to help my clinics with their marketing. I would show them exactly what to do with their marketing. I would show them how to lay their websites out for the best conversion and to have a powerfully compelling message. How to do their "about page" so it converts and hooks people in. And......none of them followed it. I was perplexed. I didn't understand it. I understood only after I did neurolinguistic programming and hypnosis and explored human psychology more.

It isn't about them having the tools. It is about the individual having the courage and the ability to overcome the fear that determines their actions. Most people try to change their actions first, which I initially did with my clinics. The thoughts you consistently have imprint on your brain, and over time they become a belief. A belief is something you have repeatedly thought. It doesn't make it true. So, beliefs that you are not good enough or smart enough are just made up. They aren't true at all. Our beliefs about ourselves and our abilities determine what actions we take or don't take. This is what determines the output or results. It is what drew me to coaching because without this mindset shift and belief shift, it didn't matter what I did. The client would fail.

Your peer group are your biggest influence on how far you grow and elevate. There is an expression that you become like the five people you hang around the most. It is like osmosis.

So, can you change the brain? Absolutely.

You can rewire the brain for success because the brain is malleable. The ability for the brain to be rewired is called neuroplasticity. Many modalities can change the brain's "wiring and firing". My favourites are vision boards and hypnosis. These are the two things that have catapulted my business growth.

## Vision Boards.

Vision boards are another way to prime the brain for success and redirect the subconscious. Swart, a neuroscientist who has worked with major companies like KPMG, LinkedIn and Samsung, says, "Looking at vision board images can make your brain notice opportunities that might otherwise go unnoticed. That's because the brain has a process called "value tagging," which imprints important things on the subconscious mind and filters out unnecessary information. We assign a higher 'value' to images than words written, and the more we look at them, the more important they become". Vision boards prime your brain to look for opportunities.

Vision boards have been a crucial part of my business success. Every single thing I have put on my vision board has come to life and manifested. I have never worried about how it is going to happen. I just focus on the end result I am after and miraculously opportunities just fall in my lap, and I simply take the necessary steps to ensure these opportunities turn into business opportunities that pay.

I have used vision boards for actual objects but also for business ideas and concepts. I have done them for product development as well. When I do this I declare what I have developed in advance as though it has already happened. Without fail, I have always created a product that is the solution exactly as my vision board predicts. It is almost like the crystal ball of my future.

## Hypnosis.

Hypnosis is my favourite brain priming technique. Hypnosis is a technique that can be used to prime the brain. It activates certain parts of the brain by using specific words, phrases or images. The use of hypnosis has been documented as far back as ancient Egypt and Mesopotamia in texts such as the Ebers Papyrus (1550 BCE) and the Edwin Smith Papyrus (c. 1600 BCE).

When someone undergoes hypnosis, their brain waves slow down, their breathing becomes slower and they become more open to suggestions. Hypnotherapy can be used to help people with specific conditions such as anxiety or insomnia. It can also be used to help people quit smoking or lose weight through positive suggestions.

When I first started my brand, my belief in myself was limited. I used hypnosis recordings to rewrite my subconscious. I had a lot of programming from my childhood, and my money story was that of poverty. My father had been a priest from a very early age, and my mother became a priest shortly after I gave birth to my first child. My childhood was one of second-hand clothes and embarrassment on free dress days. I only got $2 in pocket money, and my friends got $20. Everywhere I looked, the fact that our family didn't have money was shown to me.

I used to think that wealth was for other people. It was only after I started rewiring my thought patterns with hypnosis that my results started changing. I could hear the hypnosis audios in my head even when I wasn't listening to them. For months I listened daily to these recordings and it became so automatic that I started to believe it. The moment I started believing it my results started changing because my actions started changing.

Priming is a technique that can be used to prepare the brain for success. The idea of priming the brain was first introduced by psychologist and social psychologist Stanley Schachter in 1962.

He believed that priming could be used to change how someone perceives something or how they behave in response to something.

It is a technique that has been used in many different fields from advertising to sports. Priming is the process of preparing the brain for success before it acts. Priming can be done consciously or unconsciously. Conscious priming is when you are aware of what you are doing and want to ensure your brain is ready for it, while unconscious priming happens without you even noticing. Priming can also be applied to everyday life.

Priming has been shown to help people perform better in various tasks by increasing their motivation and self-confidence. Priming can be done through many different methods such as words, images or sounds. It is usually done with the intention of influencing someone's thoughts and behaviours.

We get bombarded with so much data and information daily that it would be too much for the brain to process, so it filters out what is not essential and prioritises what is important. By doing this exercise you light up this part of your brain, ensuring your mind is on alert to find opportunities you did not see before.

Consciously priming the brain can be done in the following ways:

**Repetition.**
Repetition priming the brain is a phenomenon that happens when an individual is exposed to one stimulus, then later they are exposed to a second stimulus. The second stimulus will be processed more efficiently than it would have been had it not been primed. The repetition priming of the brain theory is not a new concept, as it

has been observed for centuries. It was first studied by Francis Bacon in 1625 and then later by Hermann Ebbinghaus in 1885.

In the early 1990s, Elizabeth Loftus and John Palmer conducted a study on repetition priming in which they showed participants slides of traffic signs in various locations. After this, they were asked to identify the signs when shown a new set of slides. The results showed that participants were much more likely to identify signs immediately, after having seen them previously. This effect was even stronger for people who had seen the sign in another location.

The effect of repetition priming can occur both consciously and unconsciously. Advertisers have used it for years by repeating their product's name repeatedly to get customers to buy their product without even realising it.

Affirmations are an excellent example of repetitive priming of the brain. The idea is that when you repeat something it becomes more ingrained in the brain. The more often an individual repeats a word, phrase or sentence, the more likely it will come to mind. Our self-talk is one of the most significant affirmations we give ourselves; for many, it is negative.

**Association**.

Association occurs when two words are related in some way, and they become much easier for us to process together than if they were presented separately. The way we remember things is by association. This is because when you associate two things, they will be easier to access in your mind. Therefore, at school they had memory jingles. I remember having to remember the solar system and the planets. Our jingle was, "My very easy memory jingle seems useful naming planets". The first letter of each word was the beginning letter of each planet. It represented Mercury, Venus, Earth, Mars, Jupiter Saturn, Uranus, Neptune and Pluto. When we associate music or song with an acronym it enhances our ability to remember. This tactic is also used successfully in advertising.

## Writing Down Your Goals.

There is something about writing down your goals that gravitates the universe into action. The pull and power are even more potent when you also write why you must achieve them. Write down your goals and when they are going to be achieved. Look at them daily and as you look at them, imagine that they are already achieved and feel the emotion of this. Initially, you may feel silly but trust the process and keep going.

According to Dr Gail Matthews, a professor of psychology at Dominican University in California, writing down her goals makes her 42 per cent more likely to achieve them. The more you attach importance to a thought the more your subconscious will pay attention to it. When you think about your goals, write them down and connect your feelings and emotions to your goals, your subconscious mind realises that it matters.

Explaining why a goal should be achieved gives it even more spiritual meaning. When you set a goal that you're really passionate about, a goal that you have a big "why" to achieve, it activates the nucleus accumbens (NAc) and a part of the brain called the insula. These are associated with the brain's motivational centers, which produce "feel good" hormones like dopamine. Through emotion and repetition, you can direct your subconscious focus.

As you probably know, your subconscious mind controls most of your actions. Once you realise what you're putting into your subconscious mind, your brain begins training for success.

## Selling Is Being Of Service

If you want to be able to sell successfully you will have to address the money story you have going because this story is the filter you see everything through. Sales is simply a mindset and many people have limiting beliefs about selling. The first mistake they make is they judge their customers' ability to afford something. This is often filtered through their own value system of whether they would pay that amount of money. Some people pay $5 for a coffee daily, yet I would never do that. I think it is a waste of money. I would instead put that $25 towards something else. However, I am smart enough to realise that regardless of what I think, people spend money on coffee every single day. Don't judge your customers, and don't assume they are broke. Assuming they are broke is insulting to them.

For most, their hang-up with sales is simply rejection. At some point in their life they have been rejected and the pain of rejection is worse than the gain they get by helping someone and making money. They see a sales rejection as a personal rejection when it is simply a rejection of the product or idea at that point in time. It isn't a no. It is a no at that moment. There have been plenty of times I have said not now in business. The timing isn't right for us.

What helped me with sales is seeing it instead as serving someone. I came to realise that sales is getting someone out of pain. By selling, I was helping solve a problem. Putting a different perspective on sales made it easy to sell. Those who have trouble selling are also usually in service industries and they are typically people who have an empathic nature and are very caring.

Imagine your mother is in pain and you know you have the solution. Would you hold back offering it to her if it was expensive? The answer is - absolutely not. You wouldn't care what the cost was. You would just want her out of pain. Think of sales the same way because your customer feels that same pain. It affects every level of their self-confidence and keeps them up at night. They may not be declaring it out loud, but their struggle will be real.

# CHAPTER SIX

— Unlocking The Sales Superstar In You —

# CHAPTER SIX

— Unlocking The Sales Superstar In You —

Your ability to sell is directly tied to your beliefs around money and selling. We are not born with money beliefs. No baby is born and thinks anything is expensive. This is a program that is installed into the subconscious from repetition. As a child, you took on the emotions, thoughts and beliefs of your parents and environment. You may have been told, "We can't afford that," or the common, "Money doesn't grow on trees" during your childhood. These statements reflect your parents' beliefs and are in no indication a reflection of what you can achieve.

Examples of limiting beliefs around money are:
- Money can't buy happiness.
- You burn prosperity candles.
- You must work hard for money.
- I am no good with credit cards.
- I will lose my friends if I have too much money.
- I don't know enough to invest.
- I never have enough money.
- The rich get richer and the poor get poorer.
- Rich people are greedy.
- I don't deserve more money.
- More money equals more problems.
- Money needs to be held onto.
- I can't make money from my passion.
- You must have money to make money.

All of these are limiting beliefs surrounding money and they will dictate how you behave. Let's examine these in more detail to see how they could appear in your life.

Money can't buy happiness is one of the biggest myths out there. I certainly wasn't happy when I was broke, and I am indeed a lot happier now that we can pay for things. The lack of money is one of the biggest causes of marital breakups and fights. Whilst money won't guarantee happiness, it gives you a choice.

Without money you can't have the surgery that you need. Without money you can't buy clothes or food. When you don't have money you don't have the same ability to make choices. Whilst it won't guarantee happiness, it makes your life a lot easier and reduces stress. The belief that money won't buy you happiness implies that you will be unhappy by chasing it. This isn't necessarily true. This false belief keeps people broke and struggling. Money is earnt in direct proportion to the value you bring to the world, the problems you solve and your belief in your worth.

Many people avoid accumulating wealth because they believe they must work hard to achieve it. Working even longer hours is less than appealing if they already work long hours. At one point I shrank my dreams because I was already working 70 hours a week and the idea of pushing myself even more was something I just couldn't bring myself to do. The challenge was me. It was the way I was thinking. I should have put someone else on who was better at my activities so that I could play in my genius zone. It took me a long time to learn this lesson.

There is undoubtedly work to be done. Nobody becomes a millionaire by meditating on a mountain top. It isn't about working harder, it is about working smarter.   If you are trading your time for money you probably are working hard. It is about leveraging your time so you are not exchanging hours for dollars. There are only so many hours in a day; eventually your ability to earn income will cap out. Being self-employed limits you. You have literally just bought yourself a job, and many self-employed business owners would earn more money working for someone.

I once had someone tell me they had a prosperity candle. The belief was that money would come in when they burnt the candle. I asked the person, "So, do you burn it every day?" She responded, "Oh no, I don't want to waste it!" I was dumbfounded. I responded, "So you don't want wealth regularly then?" The moment I said it, the person realised what she was doing. When a person has a poverty mindset they subconsciously reject wealth. Therefore they continue to struggle because they literally repel money. Deep down in her subconscious this client did not believe that she was worthy of wealth. Yet she absolutely was worthy.

If you believe in Talismans, you are placing your power for results outside yourself. You are literally giving away the power you have to create your dreams. It means you are making yourself powerless. We are powerful beyond our wildest dreams. That power only comes from directing our subconscious mind and imprinting it regularly so the subconscious knows what to pay attention to.

*"Our deepest fear is not that we are inadequate. Our deepest fear is that we are powerful beyond measure. It is our light, not our darkness that most frightens us. We ask ourselves, 'Who am I to be brilliant, gorgeous, talented, fabulous?' Actually, who are you not to be? You are a child of God. Your playing small does not serve the world. There is nothing enlightened about shrinking so that other people won't feel insecure around you. We are all meant to shine, as children do. We were born to make manifest the glory of God that is within us. It's not just in some of us; it's in everyone. And as we let our own light shine, we unconsciously give other people permission to do the same. As we are liberated from our own fear, our presence automatically liberates others."*

**Marianne Williamson, A Return to Love: Reflections on the Principles of "A Course in Miracles"**

The expression "the rich get richer and the poor get poorer" is a classic example of someone rejecting wealth. It implies that someone getting rich is somehow taking wealth away from someone else. This is the falsest statement I have ever heard. It also implies a limit to what people can earn, which there isn't. This thinking does not serve you as a person or a business owner. It is a self-defeating belief.

According to Forbes' wealthiest list, most billionaires are self-made. They didn't inherit their money. They created their wealth. As much as the rich make and find new ways to earn money, so can the poor. I grew up with little money. I borrowed clothes and shopped at St Vincent De Paul and thrift shops. Yet despite my childhood and lack of money, I built a multi-million-dollar business in three countries.

Another false belief is that money needs to be held onto. I remember growing up with my parents saving for a rainy day. What a horrible reason to save. They literally were expecting disasters. What if perhaps you were not saving for a rainy day but saving for when opportunity meets you? How different does that feel energetically? The two are polar opposites. One is preparing for growth and the other is retracting energy.

So how do you change this money story? The first step is realising that you have a money story. All of us do. The money story changes as your business and income grows.

The second step is getting crystal clear on what you want to achieve and why. Until you are crystal clear about the type of life you want and why you want it then it will elude you. If you don't know what you want, how will you know when it shows up? You won't recognise it.

Allow yourself to dream, I mean really dream. What would you ask for if you knew you couldn't fail? Often we play small because we don't think it is possible. I know that at one point I had a boat on my vision board but I took it off. I rationalised that I didn't need it. Rationalisation is your brain literally rationalising lies. I was lowering my dream instead of increasing my vision and belief. We now have a boat, something I initially thought was impossible.

The subconscious is only changed by repetition and impressing it daily. When you first start this process you will feel like a fraud. Just keep going with the affirmation, hypnosis or vision board; over time you start to believe it and your money beliefs shift. Know, however, that one mountain's top is the bottom of another. As you grow with each leap you will again face your limiting beliefs around money, which is okay. With awareness, you can change them.

## Becoming Successful At Sales

If you are in business you'd better be able to sell like your life depends on it, and if you can't sell effectively, you need to learn. Everyone can sell. Often people tell me, "But I am no good at sales". If you have ever been in any relationship, whether a friendship or a romantic one, you can sell. We are selling ourselves from the moment we are born. The people who have issues selling are the same people with a money story that keeps them trapped.

Belief in both you and the product you are selling is crucial. Many salespeople do have ethics despite the perception. If you don't believe in yourself it doesn't matter how good the product is; you are not going to be successful in sales. A customer needs to "borrow" the belief about a product from the salesperson until they gain their own belief in the product.

Sales is more than listening to the customer's problem and matching them with a product or service that will solve their issue. Why would you not want to help someone? Because selling is simply problem-solving.

What generally happens is that most salespeople "choke" when the item is more expensive than they would typically pay for a product. They sell to customers through the lens of their own money values and wallet rather than allowing the customer to choose for themselves. If what you are selling solves their problem, then proudly present it.

When I had chronic pain I would have paid anything to eliminate it. I bought many gadgets and device hoping they would solve the constant pain that drained my energy. They partially relieved it but never fully. Do you realise that your customers are in the same emotional pain? Why would you not want to end that pain by helping them with a solution? If you know the product you are selling works, you should be shouting it from the rooftops. If you have a product that genuinely impacts lives, you have a moral obligation to get it out to the world.

---

*"Selling is a service. You are getting someone out of pain."*
**Jacine Greenwood**

---

I have been told the way I sell is different. Nobody taught me how to sell effectively; I have always just been able to. First, start by actually building rapport. The first step to building rapport is to establish a connection. This connection can be made by talking about things that are relevant to the customer and that they are interested in. The next step is to build trust with the customer, which can be done by demonstrating your expertise and knowledge in the field. Finally, you should establish a relationship with the customer by being personable and friendly while maintaining professionalism.

Building rapport is an essential aspect of sales because it allows you to understand better what the customer wants from you and how you can provide them with what they want. Rapport also makes it easier for customers to buy from you because they feel more comfortable with you as a salesperson.

Start by taking a genuine interest in them and if you have had a similar problem, share your experience dealing with it. If you haven't had the same problem but have helped someone else overcome this problem, then share that story. Stories are the easiest way to sell because storytelling has existed since the beginning of time. This is one of the things I tell my clinic owners. Don't share your qualifications; share your story and what made you go into business. It makes you relatable and makes the customer realise you are genuine.

Listen to what the customer says and take note of the words and language they use. Listening is crucial to building rapport. If a client has a problem with their skin, I listen to what they want to change. I also then ask them why they want to change it. How does it make them feel? Most people are too afraid to ask this, but people don't buy on logic; they buy emotionally and tapping into your customer's feelings is crucial to push them over the line. Remembering that you are only selling ethically and it is absolutely in the customer's best interest, so tap into that emotion. Your clients will love you for it.

Once you know what they want to change and why they want to change it you literally feed their own words back to them. I am going to give you a few examples.

If someone had concerns about their pores and they told me that they didn't like the size of them and that they found them difficult to hide. I would sell a product in this manner: "You mentioned the pores bother you and that you would like to improve them. With this product you can easily refine and make your pores almost invisible. What it does is regulate them in 3 ways, so no longer will you need to try to cover them up. Your skin will look flawless, and you are going to feel just so incredibly happy with the results. How does that sound to you?"

So, what have I done here? I have done 3 things.

1. I have fed back the very problem they don't like which they just admitted they don't like.

2. I have also given them ownership by saying you. Once a customer owns a problem, they publicly say they want to fix, they won't retract it because there will be an incongruence with what they said.

3. I have discussed how the product will benefit them using visual, auditory and feeling words. Don't talk about features. Nobody usually cares and it is benefits that sell way more effectively.

4. I have future-paced them to what their skin is going to look like after using the product. This is important because they need to be able to see that future.

Using an example of another business such as car sales: First, you would ask what the customer wants in a vehicle and what is important to them. Is it the prestige, is it the speed, is it the choice of a specific paint colour, is it the safety rating, is it the fuel economy? Find out what they want. Because depending on the customer, you would potentially sell the exact vehicle differently.

If it were how fast the car is, you would show them vehicles with a fast 0-100 km per hour profile. You would also most likely show them a sporty model. However, you could determine what the vehicle will be used for and how many passengers are likely to be in the vehicle because plenty of cars that take more than two people go fast.

When I go to a car yard, the salesperson tries to tell me all the vehicle's features. Frankly, I don't care. I want the fastest car and one that comes in a colour that I like. I want leather seats and good fuel economy, even better if it is a hybrid. Everything else is an irrelevant point to me. If they were smart, they would ask how long I have wanted this car. This taps into my emotions, and they now reinforce that I want this car. It is human psychology. Find out what they want and then give it to them.

## Your Wallet Is Not Their Wallet

Too many salespeople don't sell because they judge the customer and think they can't afford it. Your ability to purchase is also not your customer's ability to purchase, so don't judge. Sell them instead what they need. Don't sell them what you think they can afford. Because when you judge customers, they remember it, and it backfires on you. I have seen this happen too many times. The salesperson sells them an inferior product because it is at a lower price point rather than selling them a product at a higher price point but fixes the problem. It is the quickest way to lose their trust, confidence, and a sale.

Reality check – Mercedes, Bentley and BMW staff often can't afford the cars. Could you imagine if they judged potential customers based on their capacity to afford the same product? It would be crazy. They wouldn't sell a thing. So be like a luxury car salesperson.

If your client or customer can't afford it, they will tell you so. I then tell them as a minimum, what they should purchase if they want to solve their problem. I **NEVER** ask them what they can afford. Because over my years in business, they never tell you the truth...... they can always afford more. It is more that they hesitate and are afraid of not solving the problem. The more you can guarantee results and overcome their reluctance, the better your sales will be. It is common amongst our clinics that when clients say they can't afford it after just using a few products, they buy the range suggested.

## Don't Be Reliant On Samples For Sales

So many salespeople want samples of a product to help them achieve sales or travel sizes to introduce the product to their customers. What they are really saying unconsciously is … they can't sell effectively. If you are seeing the client in person, you shouldn't need it. I have never needed any sample to purchase a product. If the benefits to me were enough and the salesperson did their job well, I am convinced without trying. I know you are all screaming, "But what about the try-before-you-buy offer?" Those offers typically end up charging your card because most people fail to act in time to use the product and don't bother sending it back, so the businesses make a tremendous amount of money. They also understand human psychology because basically, people will do the least amount of work.

The only time it would be beneficial for a sample is if you already have an existing customer and want to sell them additional products and are an e-commerce business. There is then a benefit for putting in samples, especially if it is accompanied by an offer for the purchase to buy. It then becomes an irresistible offer.

If you are struggling with sales and are in business, it would be worth investing in sales training to assist you. The investment will be far less than the benefit you will achieve with revenue. The better you can sell, the more money you will make in business.

## Overcoming Objections

Most people fear sales because they fear rejection. Being accepted is one of the most basic human needs. However, when someone is saying no to a sale, they are not rejecting you. The customer is simply rejecting the concept or product. Sometimes it is also not a complete rejection, but merely the timing is not suitable for them to proceed. One of the often-missed things in business ... the follow-up. It is where the gold is.

An objection is often not real. The most common objections you will experience in business are the following:

1. I can't afford it.

2. They need to check with someone else.

3. They don't want to change what they are doing – fear of change

4. I don't have time.

5. I need to think about it.

## I Can't Afford It

I handle this objection differently if you are cold calling versus if they have come to you. If they have come to you for help, then they clearly have a problem, and you need to dig deep into their pain to help them overcome their fear because it is just fear holding them back. If what you are selling them could aid them and if they take the necessary actions, they can make money back from their investment. This works well with online courses and information. The implementation of the program will automatically result in them earning more money.

This objection is the most frequent objection you will encounter. If you delve into the customer's emotions, you may find they really do want it, but they are concerned about a large payment. Instead, break it down into smaller amounts. Ask them if they could have monthly payments and ask if this would help them. I often break it down to a daily amount it will cost them. For example, a skincare set from Roccoco, on average is around $300-$400 approximately. I then ask them whether they buy coffee from Starbucks. This is less than the cost of the coffee per day. Often it isn't because they can't afford it. It is just that they are not prioritising it enough. The way you spend your money shows your values. When you also show them that they can afford it, their objection falls away because it isn't a case that they can't afford it. It is an excuse, and it is up to you, as a salesperson, to be able to positively influence the customer when it is in their best interest.

Then ask them what amount they would be comfortable with. I have seen this methodology used many times, especially in conferences. A payment plan diminishes the fear. When they see how they could do it, they often proceed.

When a client really wants to fix a problem, but they continue to bring up price my response is this…. "The issue isn't how expensive Roccoco is; it's about how much happier you are going to be when your skin is exactly the way you want it. How do you put a price on that?"

We have seen this time and time again with customers saying they can't afford it and when their skin totally transforms, the price is never an issue again. Overcoming objections is not about psychologically manipulating people to make a sale, it is genuinely helping a customer get the true results they want and allowing them to see that their objections are not real. It allows them to recognise it as fear.

## They Need To Check With Someone

They may not be the decision maker if this is a business purchase. The simplest way to overcome this is before you start the sale. When the customer is inquiring, the question should be asked what role they play in the purchase and who the decision maker is. There is no point trying to sell to someone with no authority. It also needs to be understood that the influencer plays a significant role in purchases. You only have to look at the influence of children on parents. The children are not the ones who purchase but they certainly influence their parents to purchase on their behalf.

If you have products where someone else is the purchaser and not the influencer, you need to be targeting the influencer with advertising as they are the ones who will persuade and do your job for you in the sales process, convincing them to buy. Targeting a wife who wants something is far more effective than targeting a male unless the advertising aims to get the husband out of the doghouse.

It is important to be empathetic when a potential client says they need to check with someone. Salespeople can come across sometimes as manipulative, rather than genuinely wanting to help. The comment "I need to check with my husband" often comes up at seminars. There may be one partner who is more into growth than the other one. If the one doing the seminars is not the decision maker, then you will have issues with sales. The best way to gain sales is to give a cooling-off period and ask the customer at the point of sale will they need to check with anyone if this transaction is okay? That way you can address it and set up a meeting with the decision-maker to talk to them and show them the value of the purchase and how it will impact their life.

## The Objection Of I Am Happy With My Current Provider

Even I am guilty of saying this. For me, the value has not been shown upfront enough. I have marketers reach out all the time. They really need to cut through the noise to get through to me. It isn't that I am not interested. It is just that they haven't shown me why I need to change. If they had done some research and found out what software or programs I was using and then made a comparison, they would be far more effective in converting me to a call. If they showed me case studies of competitors, then they would have my interest.

We have got this same complaint with skin clinics. Often what they tell us is they have just had their best year ever with the brand they stock ... and my response is always, "That is what all our clinics said, and they all told us they kicked themselves that they didn't see us 12 months earlier. When can we book a time to show you how we can grow your business even more exponentially?"

My comments are not disingenuous. People fear change. You can overcome it by saying you totally empathise that changing anything in business is such a considerable exertion of energy, so you want to make sure without a doubt that you are making the right decision. However, you know that their problem isn't currently going away with what they are doing. I can say that because I know all my competitor's weaknesses and I have the confidence to call them out where they are falling down. Depending on the brand, I know how to angle where I fit, because without them even saying a word, I know they are not getting the results they want ...... and for that clinic owner, that is the most painful pain. They want to feel like a skin superstar. I just simply lean into what I know they want, and I promise them they are going to love it because I know they are.

So, if you are getting this objection, you are not showing the benefits enough and you are also not overcoming their objections. Buy into their fear of missing out. If the same people who approached me had approached me in this way, they would have achieved a phone call with me.

## I Need To Think About It

If ever there was a red flag it is this saying. This statement basically says you haven't addressed their concerns and the value has not been shown to them. The customer is either questioning your capability or if it is genuinely right for them. Ask them directly where their concern is. Whenever I say this, I want to compare functionality with software or other products to ensure that I get maximum use. Ask them what they want to compare. If you are taking the time to present their objection and compare, you are making the buying process easier. I have only ever had one supplier compare their product to a competitor and they backed it up with scientific data for the testing they did. It was an instant sale for me as the product they were selling was better.

If you are selling software, compare the cost and functionality to your competitors. It makes it easy to see you are the obvious choice.

## I Don't Have Time

Sometimes customers genuinely don't have time, but by breaking it down on exactly how much time it will take them, you may overcome this barrier to sales. There was once a course I wanted to do, and I nearly didn't buy it because I told myself I already had enough to do. Where would I find the time? They told me it only took 20 mins a day. I justified I could find that time.

If the client genuinely doesn't have time book a time for the future with them to discuss and keep following them up. I have had people chase me for 12 months before they got business out of me. Remember most people are not ready to buy immediately.

**Instruct Your Customers What They Need To Do**
When you guide your customer on what their next steps are, in the majority of instances you will also overcome their objections. One of my most loved quotes about the brain is from Richard Bandler. The quote is, "**Brains aren't designed to get results; they go in directions. If you know how the brain works, you can set your own directions. If you don't, then someone else will.**"

Have you ever been to a restaurant and been overwhelmed with the menu? Did you not know what to order? Usually, this is where a customer asks the waitress what they recommend. How do you do that on a website, though? If your customers can't decide what to purchase because they are confused, they simply don't buy.

Which direction do you want your customers to go? Do you guide them on what you want them to do? There is a reason website buttons say, "add to cart" and "buy now". They are instructing the customer on what to do.

When you are future pacing them, you want them to see themselves as though they have already purchased the product and achieved the goal they want. You can guide them there by saying things like:
"I wish you could see yourself ..."
"I wish you could experience ..."
"I wish you could discover the benefits of ... XYZ ... and how it will XYZ ... your business/life."

"Imagine 12 months from now. How you are going to feel ..."

"What do you think your friends will say when they see you?"

"How good are you going to feel when you own this?"

All of these are future pacing the client to the outcome they want as if it has already happened. Once they have that emotional connection to the outcome, they see the product you are selling as the solution.

---

*"No sentence can be effective if it contains facts alone. It must also contain emotion, image, logic and promise."*
**Eugene Schwartz**

---

# CHAPTER SEVEN

## Connecting To Their Wallet
## Through Emotion

# CHAPTER SEVEN

## Connecting To Their Wallet
## Through Emotion

Copywriting is the ONE crucial element you need to master to be successful in sales, or you need to find someone who is a master of copywriting. Copywriting is the ability to engage your customers' emotions by putting into words the benefits and features of your product or your service and why your client should be purchasing it. It has the ability to engage emotion, influence buying decisions and quickly convert your prospects into paying customers.

The concept that you need to have so many touch points before a customer becomes a client has some bearing in truth. However, the reality is if you have the right marketing message in front of the right client they will buy immediately if they are in pain and you have the solution for them. Good copywriting will get them converted immediately and will generate sales for you. This is one of the first things I learned in business. It does not matter how good your product is. If you cannot communicate it in a way that the customer feels drawn to it and compelled to buy it, it will sit on your shelf. So mastering copywriting is crucial because copywriting is your virtual Salesforce online.

You do not necessarily have face-to-face engagement with a customer at every touch point of the sales process. Therefore, being able to master the written word and communicate your message convincingly is crucial.

So, what is copywriting? Copywriting is a specific way of writing that communicates with a person's emotional brain (unconscious) and simultaneously makes sense to the conscious brain. The emotional part of your mind is your unconscious mind which we're targeting with copywriting. Copywriting should sound like a conversation with a friend. It should seem very personal. So, the style of writing sometimes flies in the face of grammar rules. It is the written word as you would normally speak it. In fact, my spelling and grammar check wanted to change most of my writing. Good copywriting flies in the face of correctness but it completely engages someone's emotions.

The fundamentals of copywriting are to agitate someone's pain or arouse their curiosity because, without it, they're not going to purchase a product. They either must be in pain or you must awaken curiosity. You need to make a promise. You need to prove that your product or your service can do it and then you need to direct them and ask them to purchase or ask them for action. If you don't do a call to action you've left your client hanging. Most people with sales, whether it be online or in person, still fail to ask for the sale; then they wonder why they're not getting the desired results.

Of all the elements of copywriting, the headline, subheading and opening sentences are the most important and cannot be understated. It does not matter how good the rest of the sales letter is or the landing page. If the headline and the opening sentence do not grab them and literally smack them between the eyes, they will scroll on.

There's a quote from legendary copywriter Jean Swatch that says, "The purpose of a headline is to get you to read the first sentence and the purpose of the first sentence is to get you to read the second sentence. If you can get them to read about three or four sentences, you have a very high chance of getting them to keep reading."

Whilst this book is not about paid advertising, one must realise that anything you do is advertising. There are some crucial components to a successful ad. If you don't do the following your ad will fail:

1. You must have a powerfully impacting headline!

2. Avoid using borrowed capital to try to market. Don't use dogs and babies in your advertising unless your product is aimed at that market.

3. Your product must be different or unusual—a Unicorn.

4. You are engaging their emotions and avoiding using brand-awareness advertising styles. You are using sensory-rich descriptions of your products, their outcomes or both. You can show them what they will gain and avoid by using your product or service.

5. You have shown the value of the product and stacked on the benefits.

6. You asked for the sale or directed them to do something. In other words, you had a CTA (Call to Action)

7. You absolutely showed how unbelievably your product would work. You have done this through testimonials both written and video.

8. You have described with such detail the situation your customer is in that they can't help but try your product.

9. You've made it easy to buy and done a risk reversal for the customer.

10. You have made them feel purchasing is urgent - otherwise known as a "Hook".

**There are 6 primary drivers of human behaviour.**

1. Certainty
2. Variety
3. Significance
4. Connection and Love
5. Growth to reach our potential
6. Contribution

Your marketing should be tapping into at least one of these 6 drivers; ways you can tap into them are:

**Certainty**

IBM tapped into this with their famous ad of "Nobody Gets Fired For Buying an IBM". It gave certainty to the purchasing officer that if they chose IBM there would be no repercussions for them. At that time IBM was known for only taking on projects they firmly believed they could deliver, and regardless of the consequences, they would see it through. They went above the money motivation.

You can provide certainty to your customers through return policies and money-back guarantees.

**Variety**

At the same time, we crave certainty and variety and uncertainty. It would be intolerable for most people if every day were the same day after day.

Variety can be incorporated into a business by offering different options, different fragrances and colours. That is why there is more than one style of phone available. Having a choice is essential. However, don't give too many options or your customer will not be able to choose which one they want. Remember, a confused mind does not buy. Only giving one choice doesn't appeal to people. The same principle applies to hotel rooms. There are different grades and rates for different rooms.

## Significance

The need to feel special and unique is tapped into by the luxury market. Anybody who buys a luxury car, clothes, watches or any prestige product is tapping into their need for significance. The purchase of these products signifies their visible and tangible level of success to the outside world.

Awards also tap into the need for significance. There are so many business awards available now and they are smartly tapping into the need for significance.

## Connection

Social media taps into connection. Customers want to form a relationship with people, not a logo. If owners of a brand become more visible it cultivates a connection with the company. Faceless corporations can't build connections.

Your business could build a connection by being vulnerable and sharing snippets of your life but only those that you are comfortable sharing. Many famous people share snippets of their life online which their fans find inspirational and exciting.

## Growth

The education and personal development industry taps into growth phenomenally. As humans we have an innate desire to reach our potential. People feel happy when they feel like they are growing and progressing. Growth can come in the form of educational growth, such as improving your skills and mastering existing skills. Personal development taps into growth by improving emotional regulation and showing people how to change their mindset and patterns.

**Contribution** – Humans have an innate desire to be part of something bigger than themselves. Contribution can show up in marketing by promoting a charity or cause, and with each sale, a certain number of dollars are donated.

**There is a fundamental process of structure for copywriting called AIDA. This stands for:**

- Attention
- Interest
- Desire
- Action

**Attention**

In order to be able to sell you need to grab a client's attention. This is why the headline is so important. If you can't grab their attention, you lose the sale. The attention component should be either inspiring them or agitating their pain point. If you don't do either then they won't buy.

**Examples of headlines for Attention are:**

1. The unknown 7 secrets of weight loss that blast away fat effortlessly and set your metabolism on fire.

2. The worst piece of advice you are following that is holding you back.

3. The #1 mistake homeowners make.

4. Closely guarded secrets of the cosmetic industry …. revealed at last.

5. The 7 overlooked tax deductions for executives.

## Interest
After you have captured your client's attention you need to retain their interest This aim is to personalise the problem so it seems like you are talking to them and them alone.

## Desire
In this stage you are showing them how you can solve their problem. You explain the benefits and features of the product and how their life will be transformed by using it. Before and after images are often used here. Your customer should be able to visualise their own transformation.

This is where you show credibility and social proof that your product works. Testimonials written and verifiable through apps are a great tool to build desire and reassure the customer. The more emotion you trigger the more resistance there will be for the sale which is why social proof is so important.

Part of building desire is future pacing your client as though they have already achieved the desired outcome. This can be done by using this framework.

Think of how (**positive emotion**) you'll feel when you (finally) (**what you want them to do or think or their outcome**).

An example includes:

Think of how you will feel (positive or negative emotion) when you realise you have finally found the solution to beautiful skin.

No more wasting money.

No more frustration.

Just flawless skin.

And a reflection you love.

## Action

This is where they sign up or purchase the product. It could be asking them to sign up for your newsletter or join this group to get access to XYZ.

This process is essential because it leads them through a logical process in their conscious mind, getting them interested and hooked emotionally. They will then naturally close the deal.

At the action stage you need to tell them the next steps you want them to take. It may be to click this button and subscribe. It could be "click the buy now button". You need to direct them to what you want them to do.

## Copywriting Hacks
## Gaining Authority

How do you show authority if you have only just started your business? When you start you often don't have the runs on the board with testimonials or proof, so how do you provide credibility and authority?

If you don't have the testimonials you can refer to your years in business or your qualifications. This can be used to establish your expert status. What happens if you are a brand-new business and you don't have much experience? You can use phrases such as "Experience shows ..." or "Evidence shows ..." or "Experts say ...". This establishes credibility for your product or service where you don't have the required credibility yet.

## Hypnotic Suggestions

Hypnotic writing and speech has been something I have been doing unconsciously. Nobody taught me how to sell, but after reading several books on marketing I realised why I was so successful with sales.

One of the things I did was assumptive sales. It was the language I used. When a customer came in for a skin consultation to fix their skin, they had an issue. I never tried to "justify" why their products were not working. I simply assumed they were not because their skin told me that what they were doing was not working. Many therapists spend their time analysing every client's products explaining why they shouldn't use them. Instead, I made the following statement:

"Obviously what you are doing is not working for you. Wouldn't you agree?" The customer always said, "Yes," because the proof was undeniable. It wasn't working. The more times you can get the customer to say, "Yes," the easier it is to sell to them. Assumptive adverbs trivialize the statement, effectively saying, "only a fool would disagree".

With assumptive language patterns you start with the statement that you want to be accepted, then follow it with a statement that is desirable.

Assumptive adverbs include the following:
Obviously
Evidently
Certainly
Surely
Naturally
Clearly
Unquestionably
Of course
Without a doubt

Examples of how you could use these in copywriting are:
"Without a doubt this is the biggest breakthrough in history."
"Clearly this is the answer to your problems."
"This product is unquestionably the best on the market."
"You naturally want the quickest way possible."
"Obviously you need peace of mind and our guarantee assures you of it."

All these assumptive verbs imply the customer agrees with you.

## Other Hypnotic Language Patterns

Another hypnotic language pattern is to subtly tie in their desire with what you want to sell them. Remember the brain goes in directions. You are leading them in the direction you want them to go in.

Examples include:
Maybe you haven't seen this yet …
I know you're wondering …
You're probably thinking ….
Presently you …
In the past you …
Remember when you …?

Some examples:
"Maybe you haven't tried Roccoco yet?"
"I know you are going to love this."
"Presently, you need help with learning bookkeeping."
"In the past you have tried numerous diets and they failed; this method has a 100% success rate."
"Remember when you first fell in love?"
Nostalgia is a powerful emotion. It can be like they are reliving the memory.

## Facebook Hacks For Avoiding The Use Of The Word You Or Your.

Facebook has an advertising policy that doesn't allow advertisers to run ads that assert or imply the personal attributes of the view of an ad. Examples of violations would be, "Are you struggling to lose weight?" The way around this is to avoid the use of you/your as much as possible.

You can change this to, "A person can struggle to lose weight". It now is not personal and if the message resonates with them they will still think you are directly speaking to them.

Changing out "you" and "your" for "a person" or "people" will allow you to navigate around this challenge with Facebook.

## The Most Powerful Way To Influence: Their Identity

A person's identity is one of the most powerful influencers of their behaviour. People will act in accordance with their identity and how they view themselves. If someone sees themselves as an "Entrepreneur" then an ad saying, "We help Entrepreneurs grow" is talking to them. This can be used in marketing by targeting who their identity is.

If someone is a salesperson their identity is that of a salesperson. An ad saying, "We help increase your sales conversion rate" speaks directly to them.

You can also use this for consumer products.

Examples include:
As a parent you want the very best for your child. This would be targeted at parents. Of course all parents want this. Once they have accepted the identity of a good parent, anything that indicates they are not will force them to realign with their image of themselves.

## If Someone Believes They Are Intelligent
"I can tell you're a person who is intelligent because you're reading this newsletter."

"Research shows that intelligent people continue to learn throughout their entire life."

This would work if you were selling an educational course that was of interest. They have the identity that they are intelligent and therefore the suggestion that they are lifelong learners will influence them.

## A Love Of Natural Products
"You feel like you are cheating. You love natural products but the ones you have used have just left you breaking out."

Think how (POSITIVE EMOTION) you'll feel when you (finally) (WHAT YOU WANT THEM TO DO or THINK or THEIR OUTCOME).

Think of how you will feel when you realise you have finally found the solution to beautiful skin.

No more wasting money.

No more frustration.

Just flawless skin.

And a reflection you love.

## Using Emotional States To Influence

You can influence sales by expressing what emotion the customer will experience when they try your product. Ironically, I have been doing this for years, naturally. I would tell customers, "You are going to be ecstatic how much firmer your skin is going to be with this cream." I wasn't being disingenuous; it was my genuine excitement that made me say it.

When you are selling, your enthusiasm will convince the customer. You can also convey this in print media as well.

Examples of emotions:

Ecstatic

Delighted

Tickled pink

Enraptured

Enthralled

Captivated

Elated

Glad

Over the moon

Excited

Examples are:

You are going to be delighted with how clean your house is.

You are going to be captivated by how beautiful your accommodation is.

You are going to be over the moon with how versatile this tool is.

Negative emotions you could use:

Angry

Pissed-off

Furious

Seethe

Freak-out

Enraged

Mad

Examples include:

You will be furious with yourself if you miss out on this unbelievable deal.

# CHAPTER EIGHT

## Creating Visually Stunning
## Images That Sell

# CHAPTER EIGHT

## Creating Visually Stunning
## Images That Sell

Visual content is more prominent in sales conversion than you might think. Behavioural studies, brain scans and tracking eye movements have proven to researchers that visual content communicates faster and more efficiently, and as marketers, we need to take notice. The human brain processes images 60,000 times faster than text and retains 80% of the image compared to only 20% of text. 65% of people learn visually.

Tweets with images get 150% more retweets than tweets without. Facebook posts with images get 53% more likes, 104% more comments and 84% more clicks than posts without images. Articles (blogs) with images get 94% more views. Image-based apps like Instagram (111 million users), Snapchat (203 million users) and Pinterest (291 million users) are growing in popularity.

Researchers at the USC Dornsife Mind and Society Center found that we often act on gut feelings—even when they're wrong. They found that people are more inclined to believe something is true when you give them a photo with a claim—even when that photo tells them nothing about whether the claim is true. So your claim is likely to be believed when you have a message with an image and text next to it. Repetition of this same image and message, even when people initially reject something as false, its "truth" can grow over time if the claim is repeated enough.

Canva has the capability of acquiring stock imagery that you can use for your marketing, however if you really want to uplevel then look at getting a subscription for stock images. Websites that have stock imagery are listed below:
Istock
Getty Images
Shutterstock
Pexels
Unsplash
Pixabay
Adobe
Alamy
Deposit Photos

Many of these sites allow you to now custom size the image to the exact dimensions you need for your project.

Another way you could get stunning images is by doing a barter with an up-and-coming photographer. We did this initially when we first started as we wanted photos of our products. The challenge with stock imagery is that your product is not a part of these photos. We bartered with not only photographers but also models. Models want photos for their portfolios and photographers need images to share their work when they are first starting. It was a win for everyone involved in the project.

If you are taking photos, don't place the object in the middle of the frame. You will have a better visual impact if it is slightly to the right. It also allows you to then put text there with the image and insert it. The photography of your product has a direct impact on sales, especially when other products are similar.

The following are tips on achieving the best photographs if you only have a phone:

1. Enable the camera grid on your phone. It superimposes a series of lines based on the "rule of thirds" onto the smartphone's camera screen. This rule is a principle of photo composition that states that an image should be split into thirds both horizontally and vertically, so it consists of nine parts in total. According to this theory, placing points of interest along these intersections or lines makes the picture more balanced and allows the viewer to interact with the picture more naturally.

2. Tap the screen of your camera just before taking your shot. It will focus then on the object you want to focus on instead of autofocusing.

3. Use HDR Mode. It balances both the dark and light elements in a photo. It produces images similar to how your eyes see it.

4. Buy a tripod. Your photo will be clear and balanced.

## Canva – The Dream Of Non-Designers
Canva has dozens of features, including a collaborative workspace, drag-and-drop functionality, a library of stock images, photo editing tools, icons, shapes and an extensive collection of fonts.

Canva allows you to do the following with photographs:
Edit the background
Smooth out blemishes
Autofocus
Brighten the image

It is now starting to rival Adobe Photoshop. There are templates for Facebook, Twitter, Instagram and other major channels. It's as simple as customising with your own text, graphics and logos and posting directly to your social media sites—this is huge as they already have the ideal dimensions pre-set for each platform.

# CHAPTER NINE

— Your Team Is Your Fuel —

# CHAPTER NINE

## —— Your Team Is Your Fuel ——

Initially, when you start your business, you will be doing every role in your company. I was like that for the first two years. One of the advantages of doing everything initially is that you become a "Jack of all trades", which has its benefits. The benefits only apply if you learn about each role you are playing and take some training in the area you are mastering. Without these skills you won't have enough experience or knowledge to gauge if the person you are about to employ or engage in the future will be able to deliver.

I cannot count the times I was grateful that I had learnt bookkeeping, copywriting and marketing. There were numerous times when marketers had tried to get me to sign up for advertising. Their sales presentation was well done and they were convincing to the uneducated and untrained. I learnt however after being burnt a few times to ask a specific question.

The question I always asked was:
Can you give me the names of three people who have recently used your services so I can ask them about their experience?

This question always surprised them. Most companies have reviews online. Regrettably, many of them can be fake, so it becomes very difficult to distinguish between made-up testimonials and legitimate ones. If a company is as good as they say, they should have raving fans more than willing to give verbal confirmation. It also showed me who I could trust and who to let slip through my fingers.

As the company grew I was performing tasks out of my depth. If you're doing a task that requires your time and you are struggling with it, you can continue to waste 30 minutes to an hour on it when this is something you really should be outsourcing or employing someone. If you can't do it within five minutes, it's not your area of expertise. This fundamental principle was taught by my very first business mentor, Nathan MacDonald. He called it, "The Five-minute Rule". He told me that if I couldn't do it within five minutes, I didn't know how to do it well enough and I should give that task to someone else.

Initially I resisted this because part of me wanted to learn how to do things. However, it's a primary tenant of my business principles now. I don't do something that I am not good at. I choose to focus only on the things I excel at. If I struggle with it I give it to someone else to complete because they will get the same task done in five minutes versus my one hour of attempting to do the same job.

Look at the activities you are doing and critically examine them. If you are not good at bookkeeping, hire a bookkeeper. If it's not something that comes naturally to you and you have no desire to learn, then hire a bookkeeper. If you are not good at copywriting, hire a copywriter, because the time you're wasting could be spent where you are better served doing other things. Everyone only has 24 hours in a day. We can't control time. We can only control our focus and our energy.

One of the biggest reasons businesses fail is not a flawed strategy, insufficient capital or bad management. It is instead the failure to invest in the right team.  Human capital or talent is the most critical driver of performance.  The best chance you have of getting the right person to help you grow your business is from the very beginning, before they enter the door of your business.  One of the biggest challenges we have had with growth is finding the "right" team members.  Over the years we have had team members who started out all right but quickly became a ball and chain, dragging the business backwards.

The first step to getting the right team members is to hire right the first time.  Initially when we were hiring I was asking the typical questions that most people ask:

1.  Why are you applying for the position?
2.  Where do you want to be in five years?
3.  How do you handle chaos?

You don't get the right candidates if you are not asking the right questions.  This is crucial because you could hire someone for the position but they will not be as great as the best talent.  We have had sales reps who just scrape the minimum order in and then new sales reps triple that amount with the same prospect.

Many potential employees lie on their resumes and pretend to be someone they are not.  The referees they give you are the ones they know will also cover for them with the lie they are telling you.  They only tell you what they want you to know, and with the questions most companies ask, this information is not revealed.

Most reference checks are useless because they are done with the HR department or with a friend or buddy.  These people did not work directly with the candidate or they have a biased view of the candidate.

Most of my frustrations with my business have been with underperforming team members. They cost me thousands, with many of them not even lasting three months tenure with us before I either let them go or they resigned. The cost to a business of hiring the wrong people is damaging. You are better off hiring slow and firing fast.

As a company we started profiling all our staff with personality assessments to see their strengths and weaknesses. For certain job roles we only hire a specific personality style. Could we hire someone who has a different personality? Yes, we could, but they will always be a C-grade player, not an A-grade player, which is who I am after.

So how do you tell an A player versus a C player? Other companies poach A players. C players are continually pushed out of other jobs. They didn't like a boss or a colleague, and in the end they resigned. That is a C player. I am an A player. I have never been pushed out of a job. I resigned because I had a better opportunity. Not because of disagreements with a boss or feeling undervalued.

**How I Interview**
Now that you know your prospects often don't tell you everything, you need to dig and get more information from them.

One of the questions I ask is why they are leaving their current job. Their answer tells me a lot about whether they are an A-grade player or a C-grade player. If someone answers that they had issues with their boss. I will dig further to find out more. I may ask, "you mentioned that your boss was unreasonable. Could you give me an example, so I understand." It is important to clarify because perhaps their last boss was a megalomaniac.

I also ask them about their previous jobs and why they left them. If there is a pattern of them being "pushed out" then they are not an A-grade player. A-grade players don't get pushed out.

Another critical question to ask them is, "What are they really good at professionally?" This is easy for them to answer. I then turn the question around and ask them, "What are you not good at or not interested in doing?" The natural response is to give an answer that sounds like a strength. I say to them that sounds like a strength, not a weakness. I repeat the question until they start getting "real" with me.

I ask for their last five bosses and ask how they would rate them out of 10. I also ask them what they would say about them. I then ask them for their details if they are not on their resume. I also made them aware that I would be contacting them.

**Managing Your Team**
The way to manage your team is to get your team member to communicate what they will complete that week and get them to commit to it. As their manager you should check with them weekly to be updated on their progress and completion of the tasks and targets they had agreed could be achieved. If they are not meeting them you would ask them why they did not achieve them. After they do not meet deadlines twice then you are automatically performance-managing them.

Another way of managing a team is to have job descriptions in terms of performance and what they are meant to achieve this year. It could be to bring on 20 new clinics. This is something they also need to buy into and say is possible. If you have their KPIs tied into their weekly tasks then they know they are not performing. After two weeks of not performing it would be time to discuss and see if they need any additional support.

I have been guilty of not managing the team properly. I was so busy running the business I wasn't managing them. It is a fatal error to do this. If your team is not performing, it is going to reflect in the revenue. Your sales are going to drop.

# CHAPTER TEN

## Defeating Exhaustion As
## An Entrepreneur

# CHAPTER TEN

## Defeating Exhaustion As
## An Entrepreneur

The term "entrepreneur" is a loaded one. The giddy excitement of starting your business gives you unbridled energy initially. Over time the strain of running a business can take a toll. Often the once-excited entrepreneur is working more hours than a regular job.

It is essential to differentiate between a business owner and an entrepreneur here. There is a vital difference. Whilst many people who go into business refer to themselves as entrepreneurs, most are not; they are business owners. Whilst being a business owner can be stressful, a business owner's stress levels can fade compared to being an entrepreneur.

One of the key defining differences is the way they think. Entrepreneurs are visionaries. They are incredibly driven. They are always looking at how they can scale to the next level. They have no intention of staying small. They are innovative, often bringing something that didn't previously exist onto the market. Entrepreneurs are out to make their mark. They are also passionate and obsessive about their business which is where burnout can occur. If you are an entrepreneur, it is essential to take care of yourself because your business won't succeed without you.

Burnout is a dangerous thing for entrepreneurs. It can happen to anyone but it is pervasive among those who work too hard or for too long. There are many reasons why an entrepreneur might burn out. They might be working too much or they might not be getting enough sleep or they might have lost their motivation and drive.

I am a classic entrepreneur. If I were to look at how many hours I work a week on average, it would be 70-80 hours a week. Sometimes it is because there truly is something that needs to be done. Other times I am engrossed in what I am doing and work is playing to me, so I never really feel like I am working. This is where the danger of burnout can happen.

If you're starting to feel overwhelmed and don't know what to do to get back on track, here are a few tips I've learned to help. Signs of burnout include low energy levels, lack of motivation and irritability. You may feel stressed or overwhelmed. I can become agitated. It feels like someone has placed a key in my back and is winding it up. When I start to feel like this I know I am stressed. These feelings are normal, especially for busy entrepreneurs.

Find out why you are feeling burnt out. For me it is usually frustration and I have been working too many hours. Ask yourself questions like, "What is my schedule like?" and, "When do I feel the most stressed or overwhelmed?" By asking yourself these questions you can examine if you are piling too much work on and not giving sufficient time to wind down.

Taking on too many tasks is one of the reasons for burnout and one I have also been guilty of. To avoid taking on too much you need to learn the big two-letter word, "No." This can be very difficult and I know I have struggled with it sometimes. However, if you say yes to everything, your focus can become scattered and you don't reach the traction you need. Often guilt can be the reason you say yes. At one point I was saying no to every social engagement and I felt terrible because people had not seen me for months. I was committed to a deadline and nothing was going to stop me from completing my goal. If I had said yes, the project would never have been completed.

Adequate sleep is your superpower. Working late at night can also disrupt your circadian rhythm. Blue light exposure decreases melatonin making it difficult to fall asleep and stay asleep. Using a blue light app, you can reduce the amount of blue light emitted from your computer so your sleep is less disrupted. Stop working at least an hour before you go to bed.

The best way to manage your circadian rhythm is to determine your sleep type. People typically fall into one of four chronotype categories: the bear, the wolf, the lion and the dolphin. Each chronotype is loosely based on the relative animal's sleep patterns and habits, so let's dive in to discover which chronotype you most closely align with.

The quiz below shows you what time you perform best when you lag in energy and when you should go to bed. I am a lion and I am an early riser. My best time is in the morning and I have an energy dip in the afternoon which is when I now exercise. I used to exercise in the morning but my energy levels were naturally high then. They drop in the afternoon. Changing my exercise routine changed my energy levels completely. It allowed me to be more productive and to be more effective.

https://psychcentral.com/quizzes/chronotype-quiz

Get into a routine and stick to it. It allows your brain to switch off. Lack of sleep can contribute to burnout and overwhelm. According to one study, people who sleep 5 hours or less are 29% less productive. If you are having trouble sleeping, chamomile tea and magnesium have been magic for me for relaxing. If you tend to get stressed your muscles will start to get tight and magnesium helps to reduce the tension in your muscles and assists with deeper restorative sleep. I bought an Oura ring 12 months ago and started tracking my readiness and sleep quality. I learnt that if I ate after 6.30 pm my sleep was disrupted and of poor quality. These tracking devices are great for improving your performance.

Find a stress release valve. As tempting as alcohol is as a stress release valve it isn't healthy. Exercise used to be my primary form of stress release but I had to find others when I could not exercise. I found that meditation helped massively with not only reducing my stress levels but allowing me to cope better with everyday stress. It also gave me incredible clarity of thought and the ability to make decisions quickly with absolute confidence.

An entrepreneur's work hours can be long, so it is not uncommon for entrepreneurs to burn the candle at both ends and eventually get sick. N-Acetyl Cysteine is one of the supplements I frequently take to increase my immunity. N-Acetyl Cysteine, also known as NAC, is a naturally occurring amino acid in the human body. It helps to break down a substance called homocysteine, which can damage cells. NAC also has antioxidant properties. N-acetyl cysteine plays a vital role in boosting immunity and it also replenishes glutathione stores and regulates glutamate levels in the brain which improves brain health. NAC improves dopamine levels which makes us feel good. So if you are prone to depression it helps regulate your mood.

Join an Inner Circle or Mastermind. One of the hardest things about being an entrepreneur is that sometimes you can feel alone. Being part of a group of other entrepreneurs allows you to realise how you feel is perfectly normal and share that within a safe space. It also allows you to release stress and emotions which can bottle up. Over my time in business I have been in several Inner Circles. Every entrepreneur likes to think their problems are unique to them but they simply aren't.

Every evening I listen to meditation to relax my mind and visualize what I want to bring to fruition. It helps decrease my stress levels and helps me relax. Develop a routine and stick to it. It helps your brain to unwind and for you to start relaxing.

Listen to your body. When you start doing this, you will be tempted to keep pushing yourself to meet deadlines. It doesn't work. You are better off resting because you will achieve the same outcome in ¼ of the time. I had to learn these lessons the hard way. I was exhausted and pushing myself. I spent three hours on an article only to have it not to save, because the Wi-Fi cut out. I could have cried. I stopped, went to bed and did it in the morning in 15 minutes. The same task the night before had taken me 3 hours. So, rest and recuperate because it makes you more effective.

# CHAPTER ELEVEN

## Creating Unicorns - How To Stand Out In A Crowded Market

# CHAPTER ELEVEN
## Creating Unicorns - How To Stand Out In A Crowded Market

To be a Unicorn, you need to be different. Seth Godin called it a "purple cow": a business or product that is so remarkably different that it is worth talking about. An exceptional product. Something completely new and innovative. That is a purple cow. Roccoco Botanicals is a purple cow. You can't grow a business to a multimillion level with no paid advertising if your product is not unique, memorable, innovative or different.

The reality is that many businesses all look the same. They are like "Where's Wally" in a sea of sameness. There is no clear marketing message for their websites or what they provide. It is almost impossible to distinguish between them, and because the consumer can't determine who is better, they will automatically judge on price.

If I look at other brands on the market that are in the beauty space, they are constantly discounting. There is nothing unique about their product. In fact most of these products are private label products from China. So, they are not even original. They get their sales by discounting heavily. To stop price wars you need to be radically different.

There are many ways to stand out in a crowded market. One way is to be unique. This can be done by creating a niche for your product or service. When we started our brand Roccoco it was started simply because of a market gap. Nobody was providing an entire range that was safe for acne-prone skin. We found our niche and gap immediately and the range was born out of frustration.

Ask yourself how you are different from your competitors. This is not an exercise you want to overlook. Most entrepreneurs don't invest enough time in understanding what makes them different. The majority of entrepreneurs can't tell me what makes them different. If you can't articulate what makes you different and it is your business, how impossible is it for customers to know why they should do business with you?

---

*"Innovation distinguishes between a leader and a follower."*
**Steve Jobs**

---

Is the product you offer the same as theirs? If you are selling the same product as others, then they will automatically purchase on price if the product's value and benefits have not been explained. Price is only an issue when the value has not been demonstrated to a customer. If you have a business that is like others, such as a beauty salon or accounting firm, then you need to be able to add value to differentiate yourself. A beauty salon could differentiate itself by giving a money-back guarantee. I can hear the cries already, "I can't do that". How much do you believe in yourself? We give money-back guarantees at our clinic. We know what we are doing, so why wouldn't we give customers that certainty?

A clinic or beauty salon could also differentiate itself by creating a unique treatment exclusive to them. An accounting firm could differentiate itself by marketing to entrepreneurs. Most accountants are conservative. If accountancy firms marketed themselves as "The Entrepreneur's Accountant" they would automatically differentiate themselves. I have never seen this advertised. If an accountant told me they specialise in rapid growth companies they would have my interest. The reality is that most don't do this at all.

Ask yourself what guarantee you can give your customers. How can you do things differently and create the "wow" effect? People don't talk about what they expect; they talk about what they didn't expect, so don't give away everything your customers get online. Hold something back so you can give them the element of surprise. I have been in multiple coaching programs. There have only been two companies that totally wowed me. The first sent me a movie poster of my face superimposed on it, and it was personalised to me and my business. I posted about this on Facebook I was so impressed. It was also a very large poster and it was shipped to me and framed beautifully. The other is my business coach Darren J. Stephens. Initially, when I joined, I got a beautiful gift which was unexpected, but then I kept getting gifts. This is what blew me away the most. They were thoughtful gifts that kept reminding me of the coaching group and were helpful for me in my business. In my entire life I have never had anyone else do this.

Innovation automatically separates you. Innovation is the creation of something that didn't previously exist. Innovation creates a niche for yourself. An innovative product or idea gives you the market edge for a period. Innovation, however, is a continual process. You only have to look at Tesla. They were the original innovators but now other car manufacturers have released hybrid and fully electric vehicles. Innovation is constant, never-ending improvement. So, ask yourself, "How you can innovate? How can you be different?" You can differentiate yourself with your packaging. You only have to look at shoes and perfume bottles to see this. Carolina Herrera has a distinctly unique perfume bottle. The bottle is shaped like a stiletto. It immediately grabs women's attention because of the bottle alone. My friends bought other perfumes which weren't for the fragrance. It was for the bottle.

Products can differentiate themselves with a unique fragrance or colour. Our sense of smell is tied in with our emotions. Our first instinct is to smell a product. Fragrance has the ability to bring about emotion. There are several of our products where the fragrance is unique to us. It is not available anywhere else and our clients love it.

Apple and Samsung have innovated by bringing out new colours for their phones. When Samsung brought out its Galaxy Note 20 it brought out rose gold for the first time. I went crazy and had to have that phone as I love rose gold. They also brought out a flip phone. This was something unique. The same consumer hysteria happened with the iPhone when they released a purple phone. Colour and fragrance can be innovative.

# CONCLUSION

You have now finished "Just Go For It – How to Grow A Multi-Million-Dollar Business With No Paid Advertising". I am sure you will have revealed and discovered some things about both yourself and your business. Congratulations, because it shows you finish things and are an achiever. Now is the time to implement into action these principles and strategies.

Obviously, as you are well aware, simply reading a book will not give you success. What is most important is not just taking the right steps, but the right steps in the right order. Many businesses take the right steps but not when they critically need to and as a result they don't get the results they desired.

Go through each part of this book and answer the questions that were asked, especially the sections on "your why" and "your ideal customer". Every other business marketing activity is based off this foundational information. Write down your innovative ideas and take daily action towards your goals.

Whilst we have grown our business with no paid ads, successfully leveraging paid advertising will catapult your business into the stratosphere. Do not dismiss the value of paid advertising as it is the only way to consistently fill your sales funnel with a never-ending list of prospects and allows you to reach new customers systematically. This book was designed for the beginning entrepreneur who is cash-strapped and wants to follow their dreams. So, follow your dreams.

If you would love to share your success story as a result of reading this book we would love to hear from you at jacine@roccoco.com

Completing this book is just the beginning of your journey. At the back of this book is a valuable recommended resource section. These are businesses and mentors that have aided me on my journey. I have personally used their services and can recommend them highly. As an entrepreneur you can waste valuable resources on outsourcing to parties who underperform. I have saved you thousands of dollars and hours as these businesses are the top in their industry and will help your business to thrive immensely.

# ABOUT THE AUTHOR

Jacine Greenwood is an international best-selling author, Esthetician and award-winning Cosmetic Chemist. Nicknamed by her customers as "The Fairy Godmother of Skin".

With over 27 years of experience, she has helped thousands of people achieve the skin they have only dreamed about. Her formulas have won numerous awards professionally, recently winning the Allē Awards for Cosmetic Innovation in Formulation 2022. Jacine is well-known professionally in the beauty and cosmetic industry for her innovation and stellar results.

She is regularly sought out by consumers who have been left with absolutely no hope of a solution for their skin issues and with Dermatologists referring to her as "The Skin Girl". A reputation she was not even aware of until one of her customers told her. She is a regular guest speaker at professional Aesthetic Conferences and writes for Professional Journals within the cosmetic industry.

Jacine has grown her brand, Roccoco Botanicals, from her humble origins at her kitchen sink, as a single mother, to a multi-million-dollar business now in 3 countries, an accomplishment she achieved whilst going through 5 spinal surgeries with fusion. She spent four years having nerve pain down every single limb of her body. Psychologists commented on her extreme resilience after her first surgery, saying that most people would be depressed if they had experienced the poor outcomes of her surgery. Having suffered chronic pain, Jacine has become the Queen of resilience and laser focus. Her challenges have resulted in her developing an incredibly unstoppable mindset. She also coaches other entrepreneurs, sharing how they can rapidly grow and scale their businesses.

In 2021, Jacine was named in the Australian Financial Review Fast 100, a list of the fastest-growing companies in Australia. Her brand, Roccoco, officially became the fastest-growing beauty brand in Australia at that time.

Jacine was then named in the Financial Times High Growth Companies of 2022 and 2023, encompassing the entire Asia-Pacific Region. This included countries such as Australia, New Zealand, Korea, Japan, China, Taiwan, Singapore and Thailand. This award made her the fastest-growing beauty brand in both Australia and the Asia-Pacific Region, an achievement she took out without spending any money on traditional advertising or social media.

Jacine is an accredited Master Hypnotherapist and a Neurolinguistic Programming Practitioner. She uses these skills to help rewire her client's brain for success, removing the limiting beliefs holding them back from truly reaching their full potential.

Jacine lives on acreage on the river in Brisbane. She lives with her husband, David, and four of their seven children and stepchildren. Jacine has 15 pets and is a self-confessed animal advocate.

# RESOURCES

"Persuasion Marketing: Discover the secret language patterns that hypnotically influence your customers."

You know you have massive potential to impact people's lives, yet your marketing message just doesn't attract the attention you hoped …. let's be honest.  It actually falls flat on its face.

You have been playing the "hope" game thus far.  You spend money and "hope" it works.  This is not strategic and you secretly know deep down that you've just wasted your money.

It is a bit like throwing spaghetti at a wall …. Sure, some might stick. Most however falls off.

If you are tired of throwing money down the drain with "so called" marketing gurus and want to finally learn how to master this yourself……….. then read on.

In this 8-week program you will discover:
- How to become irresistible to your customers.
- Subliminal Jedi Mind tricks that seduce your customers into instantly trusting you.
- How to ethically persuade anyone.
- How to position yourself as the expert even if nobody has ever heard of you.
- How to intuitively be able to identify exactly what your customer's pain points are so you magically solve them.
- The secret step-by-step process of being able to sell anything.
- The secrets of crafting websites that sell.
- Hypnotic words and language patterns that bypass buyer resistance.
- Why discounting is a path to no profit and how to sell at premium prices and still have customers throwing their credit cards at you.
- What channels of marketing actually work and which ones are a waste of money.

The result for you as a business owner is more consistent cash flow and a steady stream of paying customers who are your ideal client, allowing you to have the lifestyle you previously thought was simply a dream.

Over the past 20 years I have invested over 500K in education to upskill myself in copywriting and marketing. I learnt very quickly that it didn't matter how good my product was if I couldn't find a way to articulate the value I bring to the world, I made nothing … not one cent.

Lesson number one ... it isn't about the product. It is about the marketing!

I got sucked into paying for so-called experts who promised to turn around my business, but all they did was drain my bank account. What I teach is in the trenches learning that you can normally only learn from making the mistake. This course allows you to avoid all the fatal mistakes I made when I started my business.

When your marketing message is compelling, it is like honey to bees. It draws in magnetically your perfect client who finds you utterly irresistible. It takes just as much effort to attract a bad client as a perfect one. So, ask yourself which type of client you would you rather attract?

To catapult your business growth into the stratosphere and to unleash your true earning potential sign up now at www.persusionmarketing.com.au

www.ingramcontent.com/pod-product-compliance
Lightning Source LLC
Chambersburg PA
CBHW071844200326
41519CB00016B/4234